BLOGGING FROM THE BATTLEFIELD

They shall grow not old, as we that are left grow old;

Age shall not weary them, nor the years condemn.

At the going down of the sun and in the morning,

we will remember them.

Proceeds from the sale of this book are being
donated to The Royal British Legion

BLOGGING FROM THE BATTLEFIELD

THE VIEW FROM THE FRONT LINE IN AFGHANISTAN

MAJOR PAUL SMYTH

SPELLMOUNT

To my wife Becky and daughters Jessica and Annabel for
their unconditional support

First published 2011 by Spellmount,
an imprint of The History Press
The Mill, Brimscombe Port
Stroud, Gloucestershire, GL5 2QG
www.thehistorypress.co.uk

British Library Cataloguing in Publication Data.
A catalogue record for this book is available from the British Library.

ISBN 978 0 7524 6434 3

Typesetting and origination by The History Press
Printed in Great Britain

FOREWORDS

Air Marshal Sir Stuart Peach KCB, CBE

Chief of Joint Operations, Permanent Joint Headquarters (PJHQ)

While the nature of conflict has remained constant over the centuries, its character is always evolving, and no more so than in the field of communications. The blistering rate of technological advances in recent years has had a huge effect on military operations and Afghanistan is no exception.

In an age where events can be broadcast within seconds, the information highway is becoming a new front line. This means that we all have a real responsibility to ensure that the voice of truth is the overwhelming sound heard across the world. This is easier said than done when so much remains unverified. Trust in information is all.

Therefore, for the past few years the team at Permanent Joint Headquarters has been leading the way in the field of operational communications and they have opened up our deployed forces and made them far more transparent than ever before.

Soft power and non-kinetic effects are of increasing importance – vital even – in today's conflict and we are working hard to make sure we worry more about what actions are communicated than how to communicate our actions.

Blogging from the Battlefield is a result of that approach to harness technology and engage with audiences all over the world. Born from the Helmand Blog, which was then rebranded UKForcesAfghan, this book mirrors the content of the most successful new media project ever deployed on operations by the British military; I commend it to all.

But remember, without the brave servicemen and women who make up our armed forces and who are committed to the campaign in Afghanistan, there would be no blog and no book. This book serves as a simple reminder of the courage and sacrifice of our soldiers, sailors and airmen who work tirelessly on our behalf to build a better future.

Lieutenant General Sir John Kiszely KCB, MC

National President of The Royal British Legion

In its 90th year, the work of The Royal British Legion remains as essential as ever. The Legion is Britain's most recognised and respected charity, with an active membership of over 350,000 men and women spread throughout 2,800 official branches worldwide. It has a universally recognised emblem in the poppy, and millions of people across the UK wear it with pride during the weeks leading up to Remembrance Sunday each year.

When the Legion was formed in 1921 it had three ambitions which remain relevant to this day: to campaign on behalf of Service personnel and veterans; to provide welfare for those formerly in the Services and their families; and to ensure the nation embraced the act of Remembrance. Ninety years after the introduction of an annual Remembrance Day, the make-up of British society may well be changing, but the respect we still hold for those who serve and make sacrifices – including the ultimate sacrifice – remains.

The Royal British Legion is honoured to support this book, and the unique insights it provides. We hope it will encourage a younger generation to remember and support the Armed Forces.

This book is an example of how the rise of technology – and blogging in particular – can provide an outlet for serving personnel in the field to write about their experiences and their relationships, allowing them to feel connected to the wider world.

As readers, we are given a glimpse into the daily routines and the highs and lows of life on the front line, gaining insight into a wide range of aspects of the daily lives of military personnel on active duty – from combat, to relationships with the local population or within regiments, to issues of diversity in the Armed Forces. We view the entire spectrum of life in the military.

A comparison can be drawn with those in the world wars who kept diaries, wrote letters and poetry to send home to their loved ones. They were separated by thousands of miles from their families with only a postal service to rely upon. Today technology is helping to close the gap. While technology helps to bring them closer together with their loved ones, however, our military personnel on operations remain just as physically distant and separated as their predecessors of nearly a century earlier.

As a result, we get an unprecedented insight into the realities of life on modern operations and the opportunity to draw some parallels with our own lives. In doing so, it helps us to understand the sacrifices made by the military, and the debt that we, as a grateful nation, owe to them.

I congratulate Major Paul Smyth on bringing together this insightful and unique collection of internet writing. He has rescued these accounts from the digital realm and given them a home in print where they will form a part of history for generations to come.

ACKNOWLEDGEMENTS

It goes without saying that the greatest thanks go to the soldiers, sailors and airmen who contributed to the vast array of media operations activities over the course of the tour. Without their willingness to step forward and articulate what was happening around them, our understanding of the campaign would be limited.

PJHQ Media Ops
Group Captain Adrian Maddox
Tricia Quiller-Croasdell
Major Iain Bayliss
Squadron Leader Jason Eastham

Helmand Media Ops
Lieutenant Colonel David Wakefield
Lieutenant Colonel Rosie Stone
Major William Barron
Squadron Leader Dee Taylor
Lieutenant Sally Armstrong
Captain Philip Atkinson
Captain James Horspool
Captain Julian Allen

Staff Sergeant Stu McKenzie
Staff Sergeant Mark Jones
Staff Sergeant Matt Woodhouse
Sergeant Bob Seely
Sergeant Rob Knight
Sergeant Keith Kotton
Corporal Lynny Cash
Lance Corporal Sean Hayes
Darragh McElroy

The Royal British Legion
The Royal British Legion was formed after the First World War, which was 'the war to end all wars'. But war and conflict have continued.

The Royal British Legion is the leading UK charity providing direct, practical support to the British Armed Forces and their families. The past ten years of conflict have increased the need for that help, both today and for the years to come. As a serving soldier, I know all too well how important the work of The Royal British Legion is and in its 90th year, I can think of no more deserving organisation to benefit from the proceeds from the sale of this book.

Major Paul Smyth, RIFLES

INTRODUCTION

Blogging from the Battlefield was born out of the social media experimentation that a Territorial Army soldier and career public relations professional, Major Paul Smyth, developed while 'called up' on operations. After transferring to the Territorial Army in 2007, and having spent just six months serving with the Media Operations Group (Volunteers), he volunteered to deploy with 2 RIFLES to Kosovo in May 2008. On his return, Permanent Joint Headquarters deployed him first to Iraq and then to Afghanistan. What started as a one-month mobilisation to Kosovo ended up at just less than three years of service. During that time he has fought to bring the UK military's communications into the twenty-first century, introducing the work of the services in Kosovo, Iraq and Afghanistan to audiences all over the world via media channels that have never been used by the military on operations before, and embracing the world of social media.

From sudden firefights to the visits of royalty to the difficulties of cooking a frozen Christmas turkey while under threat from the Taliban, Major Smyth and the media operations team did their best to illustrate every aspect of life in Helmand to explain the campaign to a worldwide audience. Using the Helmand Blog, now rebranded UKForcesAfghan, everything from breaking news, podcasts, videos and stills were pushed out using blogs, Twitter, YouTube, Facebook and Flickr, but most importantly as fast and as frequently as possible.

Having created a network of channels that engaged directly with audiences, the team were able to develop content that had never been created before. While some of it would not make the pages of national newspapers or flash up on TV screens during the news, the range and diversity of content provided a unique and real-time window into the campaign in a way that had never been seen before.

Blogging from the Battlefield is a snapshot of life during a busy six-month tour of duty for 11 Light Brigade. It is a compilation of just some of the thoughts, feelings and observations from a diverse range of contributors from right across the rank range and from each service involved.

Since introducing this very powerful means of communication the work is still under way. To follow the current activity in Helmand click on to the blog: www.ukforcesafghanistan.wordpress.com and follow Major Paul Smyth on Twitter with @MajorPaulSmyth.

An Afghan guard with his AK47 at the
residence of the Governor of Helmand in
Lashkar Gah. [Picture: Major Paul Smyth]

OPERATION HERRICK 11

OCTOBER 2009 – APRIL 2010

◪ As a new brigade takes over in Helmand, Herrick 11 begins

10 October 2009

Major Paul Smyth, RIFLES, Media Ops

A new brigade along with their commander are taking over operations in Helmand after the bloodiest tour since the mission began eight years ago. Operation Herrick, the codename for the campaign, runs in six-month cycles. The incumbents, 19 Light Brigade, are returning home, having lost 70 men during six months of fighting the Taliban.

The new troops replacing them make up 11 Light Brigade, formed specifically for counter insurgency operations in Helmand.

11 Light Brigade includes units from across the country, and is to be made up of The Household Cavalry, the 1st Battalion The Grenadier Guards, 1st Battalion The Royal Welsh, 2nd Battalion The Yorkshire Regiment, 3rd Battalion The Rifles, and 1st Regiment Royal Horse Artillery. Attached to each of these units are a host of soldiers, sailors and airmen providing them with every skill set and piece of specialist equipment they need to carry out their mission over the next six months. It will also include a specialist counter-IED taskforce to help guard against improvised explosive devices.

The new commander of Task Force Helmand, Brigadier James Cowan, is taking over from Brigadier Tim Radford in a simple ceremony at the British headquarters in Lashkar Gah, the provincial capital of Helmand.

Two soldiers from the new brigade have already been killed during the past week.

HRH the Prince of Wales trying out a Valon metal detector. [Picture: Major Paul Smyth]

◤ Britain's success in Afghanistan is measured in small steps

13 October 2009

Lieutenant Colonel Robert Thomson, Commanding Officer of

2 RIFLES Battlegroup

Better security, a health post, more schools – you know of the sacrifices, but let me tell you about the real progress.

Both parents were inconsolable. They stood at the front gate of my patrol base in Wishtan, Sangin, and pleaded for help to find their child. We could give no satisfaction – their six-year-old daughter had stood on a Taliban pressure-pad IED (improvised explosive device); there was nothing left of the poor child. The parents continued to plead – a small part of her broken body would suffice. They had to have something to bury. The 2 RIFLES Battlegroup know about grief: we have seen friends killed but we had at least been able to salute a coffin. With the heaviest of hearts, my Riflemen watched helpless as those heartbroken parents returned home to mourn the loss of a Muslim child who could not be buried.

It is this kind of IED that has been the Taliban's indiscriminate and careless weapon of choice in the Upper Sangin Valley this summer. I have seen too many Afghans fighting for their lives in my trauma bay. As a Battlegroup, 2 RIFLES has dealt with more than 400 IED incidents in our six months here, finding more than 200 devices.

In my first tour of Northern Ireland in 1991–92, my platoon dealt with four IED incidents. We had nine platoons in the battalion then, so perhaps my commanding officer at the time had to deal with 36. These statistics provide some notion of the scale of the fight. One more will suffice – last year in the same period, there were 158 incidents.

And it is in the face of such adversity and such an insidious enemy, which adjusts its tactics almost weekly, that the courageous men and women of this Battlegroup have fought.

It is hard to describe the courage required to operate at all, let alone leave one's base and take the fight to the enemy. But the Riflemen and Fusiliers of this Battlegroup have patrolled Sangin and its immediate area daily to protect its people. The commitment, grit and indomitability have been humbling to observe.

The heavy cost has been recorded and rightly so – we will never forget the sacrifice made here this summer, and the hole each fallen Rifleman has left behind in this Battlegroup is enormous. I remember gathering my officers together to tell them that one of our platoon commanders had been killed. My leaders needed to know before everyone else so they could grieve briefly and be ready to lead their Riflemen back out that day.

I remember telling a tough bunch of sappers late one night after they had come off the ground that the man who made them laugh the most had not made it. The cost is perhaps clearer to our country this summer than at any other time and I am grateful to the bottom of my boots for the support we have had from all corners of our nation.

But what has not been so well told by the media is the progress we have made here. The enemy has been hurt hard here in Sangin. Many of its fighters have died at our hands. We have disrupted its IED networks and are maintaining pressure on the bombers at every opportunity. We have removed four active IED teams, permanently, and the gratitude of the Sanginites was palpable.

Yet this campaign is not an attritional one; that is not the route to progress. As soldiers, we have to provide sufficient security to enable Haji Faisal Haq, the district governor, to do his job. His area, just outside the forward operating base, is now secure. He works there daily and is much more accessible to the people of Sangin. The numbers of police have increased.

We have built new police checkpoints in the bazaar and more are planned. As a result, Taliban physical intimidation has ceased and attacks have reduced. People can go about their lives with a touch more freedom. We have opened a small health post, the first government-sponsored public health provision in Sangin. And the bazaar has got bigger. It is definitely not Bluewater but an extra 100 stalls make a real difference.

As commanding officer, I spend as much time discussing reopening the schools (banned by the Taliban in a country fiercely proud of its tradition of learning) as I do where next to go and prove to enemies that they are not invulnerable. And we have done all this while fighting shoulder to shoulder with some very tough Afghan soldiers and policemen who become more capable each month.

All of this would be worthless if Sangin was unimportant. But Sangin is important and has a significance at the provincial, regional and national level. The town is a political centre with reach to Kabul; the tapestry of tribes here in the Upper Sangin Valley has an echo in Kabul. Its market, which supplies the whole of the Upper Sangin Valley, is a vital commercial centre. For the drug barons, Sangin is a gateway that helps to fund the Taliban and their terrorism. And the Taliban use Sangin as a route along which to infiltrate fighters, IEDs and technology further south into Helmand. The Taliban will continue to fight us here in the coming months. As a result, our work has been not just important and urgent but full of purpose.

Success has not been glamorous – as soldiers in Sangin, we talk of edging forward, taking small but essential steps in the right direction. This battle is not one we have lost nor are we losing. There is much to do but as I take my gang of extraordinary men and women home, I know that the baton in Sangin has not been dropped (nor is it likely to be) and we have played our part in the security challenge of our generation that, for the UK and this region, we must tackle. And, in a small way, we have helped to improve the lives of impoverished Afghans of Sangin. It has been the campaign of our lives.

⬆ Pushing equality in Helmand

14 October 2009

Sergeant Isabella McManus, Ministry of Defence Police

[The first British female police officer in Helmand has helped to boost the number of women who want to join the Afghan national police in the area. Sergeant Isabella McManus decided to give herself a new challenge and volunteered to serve in Helmand as a mentor and adviser to the local force.]

A total of 13 women have joined the police force in Helmand and today four of them started a two-month police training course in Kabul – the first time that women from the province have attended the course. It wasn't my job to start mentoring the women specifically but they struck a chord with me. They were ignored entirely at the police headquarters and it wasn't right.

They needed a uniform giving them some status and they needed training and equipment. I've fought those battles for

MOD Police Officer Isabella McManus trains female Afghan National Police members to use the Sig Sauer 9mm pistol. [Picture: Cpl Steve Wood]

them every step of the way and we are getting somewhere. The women are empowered and it's great to see. These women police officers have classroom lessons and training on firing ranges and they are real crack-shots but working in 50 degree heat is very testing.

They face the same dangers as their male counterparts and have earned a justified reputation for their bravery. Many have had to arrest armed suspects and one lady has stopped two suicide bombers while policing public events.

In addition to facing these dangers, the female officers must contend with the views of some in Helmand's conservative society, who criticise them for having jobs. I have huge respect for these very courageous women.

◼ Initial thoughts after the first week in Helmand

17 October 2009

Brigadier James Cowan, Commander Task Force Helmand,

11 Light Brigade

On 10 October Brigadier Tim Radford and 19 Light Brigade completed their tour in a short, simple military parade here in Lashkar Gah. After 2 years of preparation and training it's finally good to get going.

The key theme of the tour will be one of consolidation. This does not mean inactivity, far from it. It means understanding that our 6 months is but the next phase in a campaign; recognising we will not defeat this insurgency in our time here, but that we will move the campaign forward.

We will sustain this counter-insurgency campaign's continuity, driving on hard to meet General McChrystal's imperative for change and passing to our successors, as 19 Brigade have done to us, a situation even further along than we found it.

Back home, I sense there is some lack of awareness of the words we use and what they really mean in Helmand. For example:

The first is 'counter-insurgency'. A counter-insurgency conflict is fundamentally different from normal war because in an insurgency it is the people, in this case the Afghans, who will decide who succeeds.

We will not prevail by simply killing insurgents. Instead it is the will and support of the Afghans which is the prize for both sides. Protecting them from the insurgent is our mission and every action we take must be to gain and maintain the support of the people.

That does not mean we will not seek out, confront and capture or kill those who are irreconcilable. We will kill only when we must. Part of our task is to demonstrate to the Afghan people that we use such force in support of them and their security. The Taliban cannot defeat us militarily but we can defeat ourselves if we alienate the people.

The second example is what I mean when I talk of 'we' and 'us'. I am not talking only of the men and women of 11 Light Brigade. The British Military is most definitely not the only force in Helmand fighting this counter-insurgency. Broadly there are three other groupings.

First, the Afghans, the men of the Afghan National Army and the men and women of the Afghan National Police in particular, the people to whom this land belongs.

Secondly, our allies. There are 11,000 United States Marines of Task Force Leatherneck operating alongside us in Helmand, responsible for the bulk of the province's landmass and about 30% of the population.

Within Task Force Helmand, under my command, are soldiers of one of our staunchest European allies of recent years, the Danes. From the Balkans to Iraq and now here in Helmand they have soldiered with us. They are here with us today. With an Armoured Battlegroup, they hold one of the absolutely key areas in Helmand around the town of Gereshk, just to the north of Lashkar Gah, the provincial capital from where I write.

There are also Estonians with an Armoured Infantry company embedded in the Grenadier Guards Battlegroup. We even have a troop of Australian gunners on exchange with 1 Regiment, Royal Horse Artillery.

But it is the third group who don't get deserved recognition: the men and women of the Provincial Reconstruction Team (PRT), the civil-military mission staff. There are 91 civilian, 94 military and 27 police mentor multi-national staff acting as the single PRT for all of Helmand, including the Task Force Leatherneck area, and based in Lashkar Gah and 7 districts of Helmand's 13.

Their work is utterly fundamental to success in this counter-insurgency: without the security brought by ISAF and Afghan security forces, the PRT cannot move forward with its governance, reconstruction and redevelopment, 'Rule of Law', socio-economic, agricultural and counter-narcotics programmes, channelling international aid into progress. Yet equally, without the vigorous pursuit of such PRT programmes in the security 'space' achieved by ISAF and Afghan security forces, such security would have little hope of enduring.

◣ Humbled by his Riflemen

30 October 2009

Lieutenant Colonel Robert Thomson, Commanding Officer of

2 RIFLES Battlegroup

When we were told in 2008 that we would become the Battlegroup responsible for the town of Sangin and the Upper Sangin Valley, we were only too well aware of the challenge that lay ahead.

Having deployed each and every year over the last ten years, we had the right operational experience but there was not one

iota of complacency as we headed out to Afghanistan on our toughest assignment yet.

Lieutenant Colonel Robert Thomson with Major Karim of the Afghan National Army.

We have a saying in the Battlegroup that one is only as good as the next operation so, as we grabbed our rifles, body armour and packs, we knew we would be called upon to strain every sinew over six hard months. We were not wrong.

Our area of operations, the patch, was about the same size as Dorset, approximately 2,225km², a massive area for a Battlegroup numbering 1,100 soldiers; there were over 25 different cap badges represented in our ranks including the RAF and one sailor! A Company 2nd Battalion The Royal Regiment of Fusiliers joined the Battlegroup to make us five Companies strong.

The Battlegroup was focused on the town of Sangin which has a population of 20,000 people, all living on the equivalent of about \$2 per day. Life for the Afghans is harsh. Most are farmers or bazaar stallholders. Electricity, while limited, is improving and water all comes out of a well.

But the people of Sangin are as clever and committed as anywhere else and are determined to build a future for their children, free from the Taliban and its horrific threats.

The threat this summer has been growing rapidly. The enemy knows he loses when he fights us openly so he has resorted to indiscriminate and lethal improvised explosive devices (the infamous IED), which also kill and maim innocent locals.

So, the enemy has planted IEDs in a greater number than ever before, trying to restrict our movements. It has been a hard battle but the Riflemen have found more than 200 IEDs across the Area of Operations.

We have targeted the bomb-maker in his home and in his factory and when he is putting the IED in the ground.

Since the end of July, we managed to kill four IED teams who were laying IEDs. It is difficult to describe accurately the intensity of this fight. When on patrol, everyone is fixed on the job in hand. The Rifleman operating the Vallon metal detector literally holds the lives of his comrades in his hands.

One of my Riflemen has found 19 IEDs whilst on patrol. This extraordinary job is made more difficult by the heat (temperatures have been above 40 for most of our tour) and the weight we all carry (most hump over 40kg around on their back when on patrol). It is not a job for the faint-hearted.

Furthest to my north was I Company at Kajaki Dam, a stunningly beautiful and striking place, but one which harboured a lethal enemy.

I Company faced a largely conventional fight to keep the enemy from the strategically important dam that delivers electricity to the entire Upper Sangin Valley.

Coming south and only 7km north of the Sangin District Centre (DC), home to the District Governor, is forward operating base (FOB) Inkerman, home to the men and women of B Company. FOB Inkerman is critical to interdicting the routes of the enemy as they try to infiltrate into Sangin from the enemy bases in the Upper Sangin Valley.

B Company has fought fiercely with a tenacious enemy who combine improvised explosives with small arms fire ambushes.

Sangin DC and the town centre was protected by A Company, the Afghan National Army and the Afghan National Police, all based out of FOB Jackson, which sits on the banks of the wide-flowing Helmand River.

Here, military operations seek to protect the people and prevent the enemy from getting its grip on the town centre.

A British Stabilisation Advisor works shoulder to shoulder with the Afghan District Governor, one of the local tribal elders, to improve the day-to-day lives of the Afghan people.

FOB Wishtan, just to the east of Sangin, where C Company lived, guards the eastern approaches to Sangin. Like the rest of Sangin, it is a place strewn with IEDs and all movement is dangerous. We have been fighting a battle of wills with the enemy here and gradually we have been able to increase our control of the area and our freedom of movement.

Finally, FOB Nolay, my most southern base, guards the southern route into Sangin, vital to our own resupply but also provides a commercial lifeline for the bazaar in Sangin.

Conditions have been refreshingly basic (austere is the posh word). There are no soft mattresses, no hot showers for the mornings or nights, the most basic toilets you've ever seen and very little fresh rations. But one gets used to a simple and basic existence very quickly.

The heat was the hardest thing to get used to – one could never drink enough and I am not sure I need to eat pasta for a while!

But the true test is whether we have left Sangin a better place. For me, progress in Sangin has not been dramatic but we have moved forward, indelibly so. We will definitely leave Sangin in a better state then when we found it.

Security in the heart of the town has improved, based on new Police Checkpoints and an increase in police numbers.

Afghan Governance has also improved as District Governor Faisal Haq has moved out of the FOB and now works from his offices in the secure Governance zone, protected by Afghan security forces.

A Mayor has been appointed – a first for Sangin – who will pick up some of those unenviable bureaucratic responsibilities which make local government work. The bazaar has got bigger under a sponsored regeneration scheme.

One hundred new stalls were added in June and more are planned. The Afghan Army opened a new patrol base which has reduced the enemy's freedom to operate. And the enemy has come off second best on countless occasions.

There are too many tales of heroism to tell here, but if you want to know more, come and ask.

All of this has not been without a heavy cost. The Battlegroup has lost 24 soldiers killed in action, 13 of them Riflemen from 2 RIFLES, and more than 80 soldiers have been wounded in action.

We will never forget the sacrifice made by those who have given their lives and we are holding their families close. The wounded are in the best of care and have got the strength of character and determination to fight back – we will be in close support.

The commitment, courage and sheer grit of every man in the Battlegroup has been humbling.

In extraordinary times, extraordinary men and women have day in, day out done extraordinary things for the good of our Nation and for the benefit of the impoverished people of Afghanistan.

Some as young as 18 have taken the fight to the enemy in some of the most arduous and demanding situations faced by British soldiers for a generation.

That they have retained their sense of humour and sanity is, to me, quite remarkable. You would not believe me, but we have faced donkey-borne IEDs – it fell off and the donkey sat on it with inevitable consequences.

So, as we come home to those we love dearly, our first thoughts and prayers are for those families who will not be able to wrap their arms around a loved one because he has gone.

But they would be the first to say, 'thank you for holding the baton high, now go and rest'.

We will celebrate our return – the noise will, I am sure, be heard, far and wide, but we will also remember the sacrifice and the courage of every man and woman in this extraordinary Battlegroup.

◣ Hopes and fears

7 November 2009

Major Richard Streatfield, Officer Commanding A Company, 4 RIFLES

It's finally here, day one on Operation Herrick. It's been some time coming as I was first told that A Company would be going to Afghanistan in early January. A Company is usually part of 4 RIFLES. For this tour we are under command of another Rifles Battalion, 3 RIFLES. We are to form part of Battlegroup North in Helmand which is based around Sangin.

A Company is over 100 strong and with attachments from other branches of the Army is considerably more than that. We have been training together since Easter.

As I look back it seems like an incredibly long period of training for the mission we are going to undertake. That said, I've never heard anyone in my position say we were too well trained for the task.

The training has many aspects. Everyone going to Afghanistan needs to know how to operate safely. They need to know enough about the culture to avoid inadvertent offence.

Major Richard Streatfield, Officer Commanding A Company, 4 RIFLES. [Picture: Major Paul Smyth]

We learn a bit of Pashtu to be able to break the ice and give basic instructions. We all do first-aid training and the majority of the company are trained to a more advanced level.

And of course there is the requirement to keep people physically fit and healthy.

The collective training has been a tour of all the most delightful parts of Britain. Kent, Northumbria, Norfolk, Wiltshire and Wales – twice.

We were the second group through the new Afghan village complex in Norfolk. At times on Army training areas it is hard to replicate a civilian population; this however was about as realistic as it gets, manure and straw with a number of the Afghan diaspora.

I got put through my paces in a post-mission Shura [Arabic for 'consultation'] trying to convince the local population that we had done something that would increase their security. Not an easy sell.

I also found it amazing how much of Norfolk is irrigated in the same way as the valley of the River Helmand. Good practice manoeuvring around the ditches, wet feet, deep mud and not much commander's dignity.

After the bulk of the training was complete we were able to take a couple of weeks leave. Whilst the training is vital, there is nothing as dangerous as fatigue. Tired minds and bodies are prone to bad decision-making.

We have had the chance post leave to do some refresher training and get the administration of the company in order. We will get our final training top-up on arrival in Afghanistan just to get the latest from the guys who are already there. Then we'll be good to go.

Every father has hopes and fears. It is part of having children. I am no different from every other father in the land in that respect.

My greatest desire in this regard has crystallised round the hope that I will be able to take my son to the first day of an Ashes Test at Lord's. My greatest fear being that I will not be there to go with him.

This fear may be no different from other parents', but it is perhaps brought into sharper focus by the prospect of six months in the Upper Sangin Valley.

On a professional level it is rather different. We don't generally deal in fears. We harden our hearts against the prospect of some very difficult decisions.

My personal hopes and fears are wrapped into the same moment. Making the right decision. Through training, experience, character and enough thought I hope I make good decisions.

I will spend a good deal of time planning and conducting operations. During that process and over the course of my tour there will be plenty of decisions to make.

Most of the time the result of a bad decision will be rectifiable, yet in my profession and very obviously in Afghanistan it is sometimes about life and death.

It is an incredible privilege to command a company of Riflemen and all the soldiers and officers who will be part of the Company Group. I have got to know some of them and their families extremely well.

I know from friends and colleagues that the worst moments of their professional lives have been in the moments of grief following the death of a soldier for whom they feel totally responsible.

I hope that I can face that with stoicism and sensitivity. It is easy to get fatalistic about operations in Afghanistan but there are Companies in Battlegroups that all come back. I hope we all come home.

The summer has been sobering in that regard and the families and comrades of those serving in Afghanistan this summer have barely been away from my thoughts.

There will be many factors involved but I certainly feel that the decisions I make and have made during training will play their part. It is a good pressure if used properly.

My final hope is that the Company Group can do a difficult job in the right way. I hope we can understand, persuade and influence as well as clear, secure and protect.

I hope we can hold and build on ground that we clear of insurgents. I have no doubt that this is not just a six-month project, but I hope we can make a positive difference.

◥ Life on the front line with the Afghan Army

10 November 2009

Corporal Phillip Hodgson, Operational Mentoring and Liaison Team

(OMLT) Four, 2 YORKS

We were moving along one of the many canals in the Nad-e-Ali Valley in Helmand province when I noticed something odd. The locals we just passed all took off. So we keep a look out for any enemy activity. It usually means we are going to be under attack soon.

After being here for five weeks, we have started to notice the subtle clues that help keep us on our toes while on patrol.

Minutes later, we come under attack from small arms fire. As soon as the team hears the shots, they quickly jump into the nearby canal. The ditch is filled with waist-deep water and mud that swallows our feet as we take cover from the incoming rounds.

After 40 minutes of back and forth firing, the shots from the enemy slow down and the enemy retreats after being ineffective. After the firefight ends, we decide to return to the compound to plan for the next mission. For us troops, these events are a near everyday occurrence.

We come into contact with the enemy about 80 per cent of the time we go out.

When the OMLT goes on patrol, the primary mission is to mentor the Afghan National Army (ANA). The patrols are led by the ANA with us in OMLT supervising. We give guidance and help the ANA to be better soldiers. We don't limit the training for patrols only.

When we find time, we try to give them medical lessons and practice finding IEDs and other tactical training.

Although we're mentoring the ANA, we have been learning from them as well. They have taught us how to pick up on improvised explosive devices better and to pick up on the atmospherics of the area we are patrolling. Sometimes you even pick up on a bit of the language.

◥ The price is worth it

13 November 2009

Lieutenant Colonel Gus Fair, Commanding Officer of The Light
Dragoons Battlegroup

This has been the second time that The Light Dragoons have deployed as a Battlegroup Headquarters on operations in Afghanistan.

On the previous occasion, in 2007, we were fighting for control of the southern town of Garmsir at the very edge of the Afghan Government's sphere of influence.

The District Centre was derelict, destroyed by months of fighting as we battled to exert control of the ground only a few hundred metres outside our front gate.

We returned to the same ground earlier this year in April, once again with the outstanding soldiers of the 2nd Battalion The Mercian Regiment with justifiable trepidation.

A Mercian captain under my command had won a Conspicuous Gallantry Cross trying to recover the bodies of two soldiers less than a kilometre south of our main base.

The progress that had been made in little over 18 months was beyond all of our expectations. The area was transformed; the formally shattered and deserted DC was rebuilt and the market thriving.

Soldiers, sailors and airmen on Armistice Parade, 11 November 2009, at the Camp Bastion Memorial, Helmand. [Picture: Major Paul Smyth]

The school and hospitals were rebuilt and functioning well, staffed and resourced by the Afghan state. Where poppies had been commonplace there were now fields of wheat.

The end result was that some 15,000 Afghans lived in relative safety, free to go about their daily business, within an area protected by a joint coalition and Afghan team and most importantly led by an Afghan District Governor who exercised control in a fair, representative and transparent fashion.

Having handed the area over to the United States Marine Corps in June, the Battlegroup was at the centre of the clearance of the wider Babaji area as part of Operation Panther's Claw (Op Panther's Claw was a major airborne assault on a Taliban stronghold in southern Afghanistan in June 2009).

We defeated the enemy wherever we found him, and pushed him outside of the centres of population in Malgir and Spin Masjid.

Despite the heavy fighting, there were only three reports of civilian casualties in the clearance of Babaji and, as a result, within days of the fighting finishing, we saw the people beginning to engage with us; locals pointed out dug-in IEDs for us to clear and safe routes for our vehicles to use.

I am clear that true achievement in a campaign such as Afghanistan cannot be measured in weeks or months, but must instead be gauged over years.

The soldiers in the Battlegroup are fortunate in that they have seen what progress in Afghanistan looks like, as they have witnessed it in Garmsir.

It is mine and their firm belief that we will see similar if not more rapid progress in Babaji by the time the regiment next returns to Helmand.

As we left, the seasonal decline in fighting had begun, the maize that provided cover for insurgent ambushes was coming down and, as a result, the insurgents' ability to intimidate and attack the locals was reduced significantly.

We were winning the all-important battle of perception for dominance over the area.

Probably the most significant demonstration of progress was the distribution of wheat seed to the local farmers. In the face of Taliban intimidation and brutal violence against local recipients and their attempts to disrupt the distribution through a combination of attacks onto the distribution sites and queuing locals, over 1,000 farmers received wheat with more to follow.

In the week that we left, a local farmer said to me, 'You can see by the amount of people queuing for wheat that the people are stronger than the insurgents'.

The population are beginning to witness considerable community-level engagement and investment and meaningful direct assistance from both ISAF [International Security Assistance Force] and the Government, and at the same time see that the Taliban are not fighting for their interests.

Though the Taliban fight on, they do so within a population that is increasingly of the opinion that the Taliban is fighting them; their support is waning fast and their freedom of manoeuvre is increasingly sustained through threat and violence.

With improving perceptions of security, communities are gaining confidence sufficient to begin to passively resist Taliban infiltration and, for the first time in thirty years of fighting, exercise some control over their own destiny.

↘ Battle of wills

21 November 2009

Major Richard Streatfield, Officer Commanding A Company, 4 RIFLES

The start of a tour is always incredibly busy. Every day is a new experience.

Yesterday we held a Shura at the base. Or more accurately, we had a Shura come to us. A large group of elders arrived to protest the innocence of a man who had been arrested in a security operation. There was no doubt that they had been sent by insurgents, but they were a notable gathering.

In Afghanistan, age, gender and facial hair are all indicators of seniority in open society. Inside the compound there is alleged to be a matriarchy; outside, in Helmand, mature men with long beards get respect. It was as impressive a bunch of beards as you are likely to find.

We talked for about two hours. They are good talkers and the conversation moves at a sedate pace. 'You have the watches but we have the time' is a popular Afghan jibe.

We sat on our haunches until my western joints creaked and we moved to benches. Green tobacco is taken with care. Small globules of spit form a circle of dust balls on the ground around each chewer.

Afghans often suffer myopia alleged to be the result of a lifetime of dehydration. They break into your personal space to look closely from behind a beard and leathery skin tanned by a thousand Afghan suns.

At one point I was told that we both believed in the same God. 'There is only one god,' he assured me. We had been going for an hour and a half at that point and I felt we might have only just warmed up if the theology continued. So I felt inclined to agree and left it at that.

We arranged to meet again in three days to see if their issue had progressed.

It all appears to be a caricature and a slightly idyllic one, but it is not. The Shura had been delayed for an hour because two children, both 9, had been brought to the FOB having stepped on an IED. Innocent victims in the battle of wills.

I will not describe the full extent of their injuries, but horrific barely does the scene justice. Our doctor, medics and medically trained Riflemen worked for 35 minutes to save them. They were alive when we put them on the Chinook helicopter to the hospital in Camp Bastion with relatives. They died of their injuries there.

It is hard not to believe it was a small mercy. Their uncles returned later in a taxi with the two coffins. They were buried today.

We are left with the moral dilemma of having found, marked clearly and avoided that device only for two children to detonate it.

Herriot of Helmand

26 November 2009

Lieutenant Sally Armstrong, Royal Navy (RN)

Under the watchful eye of Kalashnikov armed Afghan Army guards, perched on top of four-wheel-drive Ranger vehicles as security lookouts, a British Army veterinary officer and his moustachioed sergeant major survey the distant desert horizon for signs of movement. Both carry pistols at their waists. This is Helmand province and Taliban country: unpredictable and dangerous.

I had joined the vet and his sergeant major as this was one of those undiscovered secrets. They had a fascinating story and it needed telling.

Captain Miles Malone meets local farmers and organises a clinic. [Picture: Major Paul Smyth]

'Here come the first customers of the day,' announces Captain Miles Malone, as a herd of livestock accompanied by human figures appears, still several kilometres away on the bronzed desolate moonscape stretching ahead.

The soldiers busy themselves preparing drugs for the arrival of the livestock. Today, for the third time in as many months, they are doing something that was, until recently, unheard of in this remote corner of the world – running a veterinary clinic.

Meanwhile, a turbaned, wizened Afghan farmer moves slowly across the sandscape on his motor scooter. Riding pillion are his three young sons, grasping their father's billowing dish-dash and each other as the vehicle bounces over an uneven dirt track. Another slightly older boy walks alongside, unhurriedly herding a flock of a hundred or so sheep towards the makeshift wire pen of the vet camp clinic.

Miles, dubbed the 'Herriot of Helmand' by fellow soldiers, is a cheery 28-year-old captain from Sudbury, Suffolk, in the Royal Army Veterinary Corps, a member of 102 Theatre Military Working Dogs Support Unit, normally based in Sennelager, Germany. He is currently halfway through a seven-month deployment to Afghanistan based at the British forces main hub of Camp Bastion.

Miles' main role here is to provide preventative healthcare and emergency care to the working dogs used to search out IED components and suspicious objects, or to guard and provide protection to the many camps where troops are based. But he has also become the dynamic force behind a new project set up to improve the standard of living for local Afghans.

His veterinary clinic, held once a month, invites farmers from the small villages dotted to the north-west of Camp Bastion – away from the Green Zone where the majority of fighting has occurred – to bring their livestock for a free check-up and dose of preventative healthcare.

In this remote corner of Helmand, local semi-nomadic families eke a living out of the desolate landscape by growing a few crops – usually poppy with its ready-made market to the Taliban – and farming livestock. The goats, sheep, cows and donkeys are prized and valuable possessions, so much so that the womenfolk make colourful beaded necklaces to adorn the cattle's necks.

'Animal livestock forms the lifeblood of these local communities. By improving the health of the herd, we can in turn have a positive impact on the health, wealth and general wellbeing of the population,' said Miles. 'If we reduce the disease state of the animals, the knock-on effect will be improved meat and milk production. This not only increases the value of the animals at market, but it increases the amount of protein in the locals' diet. If the meat doesn't contain worms or diseases which can be transmitted to humans, so the health of the local population also improves.'

Captain Miles Malone and Sergeant Major Greg Reece get ready to inoculate a cow. [Picture: Major Paul Smyth]

Giving assistance to the Afghan population also serves a useful purpose for British forces in the area: 'By helping the locals with a project like this, we build up good relations with them and they repay us with information about the surrounding area and local Taliban activity.'

Sergeant Major Greg Reeve, 39, from Upavon in Wiltshire explains: 'The economy of Helmand is 70% agricultural, 20% livestock and 10% other. If an Afghan man owns an animal, it will be more prized to him than any other possession, apart from his sons. Everything in Afghanistan has a price, but you cannot compare local values to Western values. Apart from the family compound, animals – cows, sheep, goats – are a farmer's most valuable commodity. Female children and wives come low down in the pecking order.'

Notwithstanding the cultural differences between Afghan and Western values, in an area where the average daily income is around US$1 per day, a healthy goat costing US$70 is indisputably a sizeable investment.

Miles explains further: 'A farmer may well be more concerned about an animal dying than he would his child or one of his wives. It sounds harsh, but life is harsh here. If a farmer's herd is in poor health, his family's income will be reduced and all the family members will suffer. Once you start to understand the way Afghan society works and the crucial dependence on animals for existence, you can see why a project like this could really benefit the local population.

'The concept of a vet is virtually unknown in Afghanistan, particularly in these rural communities. However, the concept of a doctor is better understood, so when it is explained that I am a doctor for animals, the villagers are more accepting. I think there is a certain suspicion of "white man's magic", however, an important aspect to the clinic is the education which we simultaneously endeavour to give the locals about animal welfare and husbandry.'

Despite the value Afghans place on their livestock, Greg says there is a staggering ignorance amongst the largely illiterate populace about how to care for their beasts: 'Farmers here have absolutely no idea about animal husbandry. There is near total ignorance about causes and spread of disease, breeding cycles and how milk is produced. If a goat stops milking, it is said to be Allah's will rather than the fact that it has not bred for 18 months and therefore has no anatomical reason to produce milk.'

As such, the natural health of herds is poor, with cattle usually underweight and riddled with worms, mites and other parasites. They also frequently carry infectious diseases, which can spread to humans with devastating consequences. Brucellosis, a disease now virtually extinct in the UK through vaccination programmes, is commonplace here and causes abortion and premature births in both cattle and humans. The intestinal worms carried by sheep and goats also spread to humans via the food chain.

Miles says the priority is firstly to de-worm and de-louse. By eradicating parasites, the animals are able to absorb more nutrients, become stronger and more resistant to disease. Once the animals have achieved a baseline of health, he then vaccinates because the vaccinations are less effective on sick animals.

Captain Miles Malone treating an Afghan sheep. [Picture: Lt Sally Armstrong]

'From a slightly geeky veterinary perspective, these herds are fascinating because the goats and sheep are extremely

ancient breeds. They have not been engineered by breeding programmes and are as they would have appeared in biblical times. Because they have not been exposed to drugs and have built up no resistance, they respond extremely well and quickly to the products I give them.

'Our main effort has to be focused on herd health. De-worming and vaccination programmes, which will steadily see an improvement in the overall quality of all the animals, will reap long-term benefits. Of course, if specific animals present with sickness I'll do my best to treat them too.'

This is the third time in three months that Miles has held his Vet Camp. Already he is seeing the same farmers returning with their herds for treatment.

'The improvement in herd health is marked, even in such a short space of time. But it is important that the locals understand they need to continue with treatments. That is where education is so important. It is not a one-stop shop and I aim to provide a continuous service to give preventative healthcare.'

To immunise and worm each animal costs around £1.70 in medication, rising to £4 per head if antibiotics are needed.

Greg says: 'This needs to be sustainable, so we ensure we source the drugs from local suppliers. We advise them on what they need to stock, storage methods and use by dates. In the future we also hope to train Afghans in basic veterinary skills so that they can be the ones treating the farm animals. That way, we hope to leave a lasting and beneficial legacy as the result of this project.'

After his livestock have been treated, the Afghan farmer shakes hands with the vet, mounts his motor scooter and wends his way slowly home, accompanied by his children and animals.

Greg comments: 'That farmer and his brother are, by Afghan standards, very wealthy and therefore influential. If we can get him on side to spread the word about the veterinary programme, I think we will have loads more customers in future.'

Sure enough, the next day several more local farmers arrive at the clinic, together with around 500 head of sheep, goats and a couple of donkeys for Miles to inspect and inject with medicines.

When all is done, he stretches his aching back, sips some water and cracks a broad grin. It is the satisfied smile of a job well done, by a man confident in the fact that he is making a difference.

◪ CO 3 RIFLES reports from Helmand

26 November 2009

Lieutenant Colonel Nick Kitson, Commanding Officer,

3 RIFLES Battlegroup

We had the great honour to take over from our sister battalion, 2 RIFLES, on Monday 19 October 2009 here in Sangin. It was fantastic to arrive, to catch up with many familiar faces and trade stories.

2 RIFLES have given much and made many sacrifices, but they have also made remarkable progress during their time here. They have left us many opportunities which we are eager to take forward for the people of Helmand.

We have assumed the role of Battlegroup (North), with our area of responsibility in Northern Helmand province stretching from Sangin up to the Kajaki Dam.

Throughout the area the Helmand River winds its way along the flood plain from the dam southwards through the mountainous desert landscape. It creates a strip of richly farmed fertile land either side of it, laced with irrigation channels and known as the Green Zone.

Patrolling is our main activity. We are bringing security and stability to the area, reassuring the local population around us and encouraging them to go about their normal routine.

As and when the need arises we will launch deliberate operations and take the fight to the enemy, clearing areas of insurgents and disrupting their activities.

We also work closely alongside our Afghan hosts in the nascent Afghan National Army and Police, exchanging ideas and tactics with them so they grow in ability and confidence in order to tackle the insurgency.

I am hugely impressed by their professionalism and dedication. We all have much to learn from them too and have much faith in their abilities.

Soldiers from 3rd Battalion The Rifles and the Afghan National Army approach a small village near Sangin during a joint foot patrol. [Picture: Sgt Keith Cotton]

Most have been pleasantly surprised by the living conditions in the forward operating bases, not exactly home comforts but certainly manageable, and accommodation is generally decent.

The majority of our food comes in the form of 'compo' rations, prepared by a small and dedicated detachment of chefs, who are always finding new ways to turn fairly basic ingredients into exciting meals for hungry Riflemen. We top these up with fresh produce whenever the opportunity arises.

The Royal Engineers are always hard at it, trying to make our stay more comfortable by improving the showers, toilets and lodgings.

The temperature is now a very agreeable 25 degrees in the day but drops off sharply to around five degrees overnight. We expect the cold weather to hit over the next few months.

Who knows, maybe we shall see a white Christmas in the desert! We shall certainly see rain and the liquid mud it will create around us.

This is already proving to be a tour that will test and shape us all. The operation remains a difficult and a dangerous one, but all the men and women under my command are totally up to the challenge.

We have all received excellent training to get us to this point and we have access to some of the best kit I have seen during my time in the Army.

◥ Welcome to Helmand

4 December 2009

Tim, Economic Adviser, Provincial Reconstruction Team (PRT)

I work in a Provincial Reconstruction Team in Helmand province, Afghanistan – part of the international mission to

support the Government of Afghanistan and help Afghans govern their country for themselves.

My job title is Economic Adviser. I work with the local government to support economic development in Helmand and help give people the chance to earn a decent living – so they aren't forced to join the Taliban's ranks out of desperation.

We're a multinational team, made up of staff from the UK, Afghanistan, Estonia, Denmark and the US, and working closely with the UK and US military, known as Taskforce Helmand and Taskforce Leatherneck respectively. I'm the new kid. I flew in from Kabul last week – so I'm still getting used to the way things work and learning all the military terminology. (To me, M&E means monitoring and evaluation. To the military it means mines and explosives. It's important to be clear exactly what we're talking about.)

Tim pictured with some local kids and a newly built bus stop.

45

Life here is very different from the picture of Afghanistan you see on the news. I'm based in the town of Lashkar Gah, Helmand's provincial capital, which sits on the Helmand River 200 miles from the southern border with Pakistan. The Helmand River valley is actually one of the most green and fertile regions in Afghanistan. But security remains very difficult, and British soldiers are laying down their lives in the fight against the insurgency. Yesterday I attended a memorial service for two soldiers from this base who were killed by an IED. It brought home the stark reality of the situation here.

The aim of the Provincial Reconstruction Team is to help the Government of Afghanistan improve security, create jobs and deliver services to the Afghan people. It's a crucial part of the international mission here. I've already seen some of the successful projects we've delivered. In the photo I'm standing next to a bus station which we helped to build.

We're providing small-scale loans so local farmers can buy land and equipment. And as a result of a US-funded project, people in Lashkar Gah recently started receiving a reliable supply of electricity for the first time, generated using hydropower from the Helmand River. Businesses can now operate more easily. Families can switch on a light and listen to the radio. Winter is approaching in Helmand and one of the Afghan staff in my team who lives in Lashkar Gah told me that he can now use an electric heater for the first time.

This is just the beginning of the story.

⧉ A day in the life

5 December 2009

Lance Corporal Paul Livingston, 3 RIFLES

It's 0300 hrs and the Fire Support Group (FSG), A Company 3 RIFLES from FOB Nolay, just south of Sangin, are preparing to move out on a Company operation to find and arrest a known improvised explosive device maker.

I am Lance Corporal Paul Livingston, a 'Jackal' armoured vehicle commander and currently acting as A Company's FSG second in command. Early starts like this are common because they allow us to move into position without the enemy knowing where we are, giving us the element of surprise. Our role is to secure a route for the Company to move along, and then using the high ground, provide over-watch to allow the Company to move forward safely to the target compound.

Not every morning is this busy. Usually my day starts at around 0600 hrs. I get into my morning routine, washing, shaving and getting some breakfast, before attending the daily operational brief, which tells us what patrols are happening during the day. This is important, especially for the FSG, as we are the quick reaction force (QRF) if any patrols need assistance.

The rest of the morning is spent doing essential maintenance on all the Jackal armoured vehicles, making sure they are fighting fit for whatever task the FSG may well find itself dealing with. As the second in command of the FSG, my main responsibility is that we have enough ammunition, water, fuel and manpower to carry out any tasking we are given. The vehicles we have are the key to our mobility, so if they are in rag, we are practically useless.

Lunch at FOB Nolay usually consists of noodles, pasta, and any leftovers from breakfast, but every now and again something special gets laid on like frankfurters or quiche. Usually after lunch a trip to the gym is on the menu. The gym at Nolay is pretty basic, but there is enough here to beast yourself with. Hopefully there will be some extra gym equipment in time for Christmas.

Throughout the day there is the usual task of 'stagging on' (Army term for guard duty), in the Sangers to provide protection for the FOB. Constant improvements to the FSG's accommodation are always taking place. The most recent additions to the FSG, two chickens and two goats, have meant that a new enclosure has been created to keep them till

Christmas, where they will make a fine addition to the usual lunchtime meal of noodles. The evening is an ideal time to try and relax. We all try and get together and watch a film or play a few games on the Wii games console.

Over the next few days I will be leaving Nolay to be a part of an ISAF operation to establish new patrol bases along a key supply route. The days leading up to this will be taken up by battle preparation, getting all the vehicles and ourselves ready for the challenge. I'm really looking forward to the operation. Once it is complete it will bring much more security to a large area and will cut down movement to the insurgents.

I wish my girlfriend a Happy Christmas, good luck with the birth, and I can't wait to see you.

[Lance Corporal Livingston's platoon commander, Captain Andy Michael, says: 'Lance Corporal Paul Livingston is an exemplary soldier. He is physically robust, professional, and cares deeply about the Riflemen in his charge. He is much liked by his commanders and all members of the A Company FSG.']

◪ Scramble

10 December 2009

Flight Lieutenant David Hirst, Royal Air Force (RAF)

It's amazing how quickly things can change here – the other day was typical of how within a few hours the circumstances can change from one extreme to the other.

We've had a fairly quiet period recently, with very few aircraft 'scrambles' (this is where we get an urgent tasking to get a pair of armed RAF Tornado aircraft airborne to support ground troops in need of immediate air support); then yesterday it suddenly all happened within the blink of an eye. The call came from the Operations desk and the crew bolted out the door shouting 'SCRAMBLE!'

Before anyone even got near the scramble bell – fashioned out of a fired-out 110mm artillery shell and a couple of 27mm aircraft round (bullet) casings – the ground crew were hot on the crew's heels and in the minibus to get to the flight line, a few hundred metres away.

Tornado GR4s at Kandahar Airfield in Afghanistan. [Picture: SAC Neil Chapman]

The crew-in was slick, having already 'cocked' the jet, a term derived from cocking a weapon, which, with a 27mm cannon and armed with precision guided bombs and missiles, the Tornado GR4 (Ground attack and Reconnaissance Mark 4) definitely qualifies as; both aircraft were 'wheels-up' and overhead the ground troops over 100 miles away within minutes.

On this day we launched the Ground-Close Air Support (GCAS) aircraft twice more, on what was anticipated to be a 'quiet day'. It is this sort of requirement that gets the whole of the engineering shift fired up and motivated about being out here.

◪ Massive Taliban bomb blasted

10 December 2009

Captain James Horspool, Royal Logistic Corps, Media Ops

We were on the edge of the Green Zone (lush agricultural land that runs along the Helmand River valley), the place where the Taliban fight is fiercest, when an explosion shattered the gentle rural peace in the village of 'Chinah' in Sangin province.

But the explosion was controlled. The area was cleared and not a single person, military or civilian, was hurt by what turned out to be one of the biggest bombs found in Helmand so far in the tour.

A controlled explosion gets rid of the threat. [Picture: Sgt Keith Cotton]

The team dealing with the bomb said it's definitely the biggest they've dealt with, 80kg for the main charge and it was quite

a complex device. It was found when I was out with a joint patrol made up of the Afghan National Army (ANA) and British soldiers from 3 RIFLES Battlegroup. Our aim was to keep the Taliban pushed out of the area.

The ANA soldiers did a cracking job. It was one of them that found the device. Out here they notice the subtle things that we tend to overlook, as this is not our backyard. The more we work together the better that relationship becomes, and just like today it is paying off and saving lives.

The single biggest threat to British troops in Afghanistan today is roadside bombs. But it hasn't always been that way. Taliban tactics have changed, as every time they take on the Brits in a head-on fight, they come out of the encounter the losers. So, if you cannot fight and win, what do you do? Plant bombs, otherwise called improvised explosive devices, and target us that way.

Across Helmand troops are doing all they can to minimise the threat, and over the summer managed to find well over 1,000 devices. Every single day troops are on the ground patrolling. But each and every time they leave the security of the bases the threat is there.

It plays on the minds of each and every soldier that some are physically sick as they head off knowing that the next step could be their last. But, it's not just us, you see kids running around left right and centre, and unfortunately IEDs are indiscriminate. Our patrols find a lot of the locals like it when we come in and destroy them. They often point out where devices are. Many of the locals are quite friendly, they're happy to see you. And they've got quite good relationships with the Afghan National Army, and they like to see us out together. That puts a smile on their faces.

But the patrol provides a lot more than just smiling faces. For us Brits out with the ANA they make a perfect team. Our skills are passed onto the ANA and it is their knowledge of the area that means they can spot the things we may not see.

◪ A day in the life of a thinking Rifleman

15 December 2009

Rifleman Phil Thomas, 3 RIFLES

The day normally starts with a kick to the cot bed I'm curled up on. It's six o'clock in the morning and I can see my breath as a cloud of mist against the dirty white of the wall in my room.

'Get up Tommo! Time for a scrape,' my platoon sergeant Tim Exley says. I force myself out of my doss bag (sleeping bag), and head down to the well. The lads have fashioned a pulley system to get the water out so we don't have to dip in to our valuable 'brew water' supply.

We moved into these two compounds about eight days previous and, with the help of an Engineer section, have transformed them into something resembling a home. After washing and shaving comes breakfast around the communal fire, the hub of the camp. There is the usual bartering over ration packs (usually with a lot of corned beef hashes left in the corner, swiftly followed by the platoon commander Lieutenant Dixon sniffing around for seconds).

The plan for the day is a routine patrol for a couple of hours and then some downtime till my team takes over the guard of the patrol base. We spend the next couple of hours getting kit ready, oiling weapons, checking comms and, for some of the lads, getting some head down (a good soldier sleeps when he can).

It's soon time to head to the loading bay, then out the front gate. Today we have the ANA with us; it's a major bonus for us because they really excel at interacting with the local community in a way that ISAF forces could never achieve, and this helps with building up the hearts and minds initiative that is so vital to rebuilding the country.

Whilst walking around we tend to attract groups of children looking for sweets or pens and, in the case of some of the

Riflemen's attempts at Pashtu (the local language), something to laugh at. It is slow and hard going, with the weight of the kit combined with the drills we use to combat the IED threat. But we have all known people who have either been killed or injured by these devices, so you don't hear any complaints.

We meet a local mullah (elder) and the boss discusses improvements to local amenities such as the mosques and schools. We head back to the patrol base and say farewell to the ANA until the next patrol. After a short debrief then it's off to fill sandbags and carry on making little improvements to the camp (a platoon sergeant is only happy when his men are working hard rather than hardly working).

While we were out, some mail was dropped off so the lads spend some time reading letters from loved ones and parcels full of sweets. As it's the run up to Christmas as well, we have started to get cards and mince pies and all the usual paraphernalia that comes with it. We'll be having the local ANA commander over for Christmas as we were kindly invited over to his base for Eid (Islamic equivalent to Christmas), where I tried goat for the first time, and for the record it's like a really fatty lamb. Christmas is a chance to have the great tradition of the boss and sergeant cooking and serving us all Christmas dinner.

My turn for sentry comes around far too quickly so it's time to wrap up warm and sit on a cold sandbag for an hour at a time, not the most exciting job but considering we're in Sangin, a necessity none of us take lightly. It's 2100 by that time and I'm glad the lads have gotten the fire going so when I come off the sangers, I can warm my ice cold hands and listen to the banter; with the lads coming from as far south as Cornwall and as far north as Newcastle (plus anywhere in between), it's quite varied, mostly at me for being the only Welshman.

By half ten it's time to hit the hay. It's surprising how tired you can get, thinking you have to do the same thing tomorrow, but as we're finding out, no day in Sangin is ever the same as the one before.

◥ Dispatches from Sangin

24 December 2009

Lieutenant Colonel Nick Kitson, Commanding Officer,

3 RIFLES Battlegroup

Christmas Eve seems as good a time as any to provide the latest update from the 3 RIFLES Battlegroup, based mainly in Sangin, and with elements up in Kajaki, here in Northern Helmand.

Since I last wrote towards the end of November, the theme has been one of continued progress on all fronts. The temperature, the reduced winter vegetation and the pressure which the insurgents face – from us and others – have all acted in our favour. We have been ruthless in exploiting these advantages and every soldier in the Battlegroup has worked tirelessly, with great commitment, to ensure we press home every opportunity to increase the security in our areas and convince the locals to reject the insurgents.

Mobilising the population to reject the insurgency is the name of the game; our Afghan Army and Police partners are working with us towards this goal. Having conducted several significant operations to establish ourselves in new, smaller patrol bases with a broader and more comprehensive footprint, we are now living at much closer quarters with the population. This has helped us achieve the meaningful interaction with them that is the essence of counter-insurgency – interaction which the enemy do their utmost to prevent. That in itself speaks volumes.

Now that we are genuinely their neighbours in a large number of places (there are 29 security force locations of various shapes and size in the Battlegroup area, of which we are present in 23), we can communicate with the locals on a continuous basis, understand their hopes and fears and tell them the truth about what we are trying to do.

This is a traditional and remote rural area with few trappings of the modern world, even by Afghan standards. Yes, there

Lieutenant Colonel
Nick Kitson.

are battered old cars (normally white Toyota Corolla Estates from the '80s containing at least 15 people), motorbikes and the occasional ancient tractor, but even the ubiquitous mobile phone has no functioning network here. The people have not had the benefit of meaningful modern education. The limited healthcare is normally in the hands of profiteers offering little but quackery for a populous that knows no better. Government services do not stretch much beyond the odd electricity line, knitted together and only occasionally carrying a current.

There are 50 policemen for a population of about 35,000; that's less than 20 on duty, measured against the sort of shift system that we would recognise at home. As such the locals are highly prone to the tallest of stories that the Taliban have to offer. This intimidation and misinformation is purely to cow the population into submission – and rejection of the modern world – for no other purpose than to retain the dominance of power-hungry extremists and smugglers with no interest beyond their own status and material gain.

By getting amongst the population and interacting with them on a persistent basis, we with our Afghan colleagues provide them with visible, tangible security and protection from these abuses. We can communicate and discuss the pros and cons of the progress we hope to bring without then leaving them to the devices of the insurgents once we have gone back to our big bases. We explain what it is that we are helping the Government of Afghanistan to deliver, and put all our powers of leadership and persuasion towards mobilising the population to reject the insurgency.

This sets us up to 'win the argument' as our 2 star regional commander, Major General Nick Carter (also a Rifleman), calls it. The majority of the people we speak to dislike the insurgents and what they bring, but they say they are powerless to resist. Our job is to convince them that only they can comprehensively rid this place of the insurgents and that they will have to put their own heads above the parapet, with the ANA's and our support, to do so. By being amongst them and providing real and visible signs of progress, we hope to convince them of this.

In terms of progress, our 'crown jewel' is the Sangin Bazaar, bustling, prosperous and ever expanding as new stalls are renovated and stocked daily. It is unrecognisable from only last year and the local population is able to go about its business there peacefully and relatively unmolested. Such is its success that it is an increasingly visible thorn in the insurgents' side, to the point where they are prepared to send suicide bombers in its direction. This is a desperate attempt to push back on the progress that we and the Afghan Government are delivering there.

The insurgents clearly have no compunction about sacrificing the lives of local Afghan civilians in order to achieve their nihilistic and self-serving objectives. In stopping just such an attempt on 15 December, we suffered the tragic loss of

Lance Corporal Kirkness and Rifleman Brown, alongside two brave Afghan Army 'Warriors' (Warrior is the rank of an ANA private soldier). Two other Afghan soldiers were seriously injured in this incident when not one but two suicide bombers on the same motorbike, heading in the direction of the bazaar, realised the game was up when they ran into our vehicle checkpoint. Our thoughts and prayers are with all those devastated by this event, but we draw immense comfort and pride from the fact that these sacrifices averted a much larger tragedy, both in terms of human suffering and our mission out here. These courageous soldiers died doing exactly what we are meant to be doing, which is keeping the fight away from the population centres so that they have a chance to regenerate and show progress that people can believe in and carry forward themselves.

That event was the start of what you will know has been a particularly tough patch for us regarding casualties. Since that day, the Battlegroup has lost Lance Corporal Pritchard (Royal Military Police), Lance Corporal Roney (3 RIFLES) and Lance Corporal Brown (PARA), as well as an Afghan interpreter. In amongst those tragedies we have also had several Riflemen wounded, some seriously. All these have been sustained in the course of the daily acts of courage and determination we witness out here. These losses are a bitter blow to us and take away highly valued and capable individuals. We have no choice but to dust ourselves off and carry on, ensuring that their sacrifices are not in vain. Once again our thoughts and prayers go out to families and friends, particularly as they and we all do our best to celebrate Christmas under testing circumstances.

But to put this in a perspective that rarely comes through in the media at home, these are our first losses for a month during which we have continued to fight as hard, continued to take casualties, continued to engage with the locals and continued to make progress alongside our Afghan colleagues.

An upturn in casualties such as this is not in itself an indication of increasing success, failure or even activity in terms of our campaign here. It is simply luck – good or bad –

and events taking their often unpredictable course in this most unpredictable of environments. None of these things stop the steady surge of progress that we are making and which gains momentum as it goes along. The background noise, the intensity and frequency of the fight, the daily routine remains largely unchanged – the difference between good and bad outcomes is often a matter of inches and seconds, as all soldiers know. We've had some bad luck but we continue to have plenty of good fortune and success at the same time.

In the past 10 days, we have opened up three new patrol bases and brought the beginnings of security to new communities yet further out from the centre of Sangin. Initially, our new presence is contested by the insurgents, but they cannot keep it up for long; we hit them hard when they show themselves and most of the population in the new areas welcome us. This is as hard a blow for the insurgents as our decisive but measured military response to their desultory shots and desperate, indiscriminate IED laying.

The locals are war-weary and want the prosperity the Afghan Government promises. They do not reject us but rather fear the day we might have to leave. That is why we also work hard to bring our Afghan comrades on, sharing bases and patrols with them as we do, setting them up for the time when they can take this on themselves. We are dominating our ground and pushing the enemy away from the 'crown jewel'. Our task is to allow Afghan development and governance to flourish in central Sangin by creating the space for it to take root.

The brave soldiers of this Battlegroup are doing just that, through thick and thin. The enemy is out there and we are doing battle with him but he is not at the gates. Fighting is less frequent, less destructive and further afield. Eid al Adha was celebrated openly here for the first time in four years, women who choose to can go about unveiled, people are moving back into their homes.

A brief mention of the home team in Edinburgh and more widely, who are doing such a great job of looking after our wounded and our families. It is a source of great strength to us here that our loved ones at home are so well cared for, whether they be anxious families on 'the patch' or those who have sadly been affected by events out here. Reports from Selly Oak, Headley Court and elsewhere about the determination, good humour and positivity of our wounded are truly inspiring and humbling.

The generosity of our supporters who have contributed so comprehensively to our Wristband Fund has made it possible to show how much we as a Battalion and a Regiment care and are prepared to go the extra mile beyond the excellent medical care already provided. The generosity and support of the great British public, manifested through parcels and messages, is heart-warming and means a great deal to us all. We shall all miss our families over Christmas but we at least have the comradeship and close bonds that sharing in this tough fight brings. Christmas this year will be celebrated with our military family – our brothers in arms.

The giggling sound of children

25 December 2009

Padre Mark Christian, Senior Chaplain

Every time a soldier loses his life we gather at our headquarters to remember them, to honour and respect them and to pray for their family and friends. Last week, at the end of one such service, our brigade commander came off the parade and said to me, 'listen to that, Padre'. I wondered what he was talking about. I listened. I could hear the sound of traffic from the town that surrounds our base, but then I became aware of the laughing and shouting and squealing, and the giggling sounds of children playing. The brigadier commented that we wouldn't have heard that three months ago.

I went to the garden outside our church and reflected on the sounds of those children. I allowed my mind to travel home to my children. Another Christmas apart. They are adults now but

11 Light Brigade's Senior Padre Mark Christian conducts a service at Lashkar Gah Main Operations Base. [Picture: Sgt Rob Knight]

I miss them as all of our soldiers miss their families. One of my daughters will give birth to my first grandchild in February. I will miss that too. I reflect on the many, many conversations I have had with soldiers about the pain of being separated from loved ones. I think of the times I have been privileged to listen as soldiers record bedtime stories for their children.

My thoughts turned to the children I have met in the various places I have served with the Army. The orphanage in Bosnia that soldiers volunteered to repair. The ragged slip of a girl that I met in Iraq in 2003. With all of the children of her village, she surrounded the vehicle I was on, to grab one of the sweets I was offering. When all the sweets had gone and the crowd has dispersed, she remained, sitting shyly on a sand hill looking at me. I made faces at her. She laughed. She slowly made her way towards me and held out both her hands. In each was one of the sweets she had fought so hard to win. She tried to give one back to me. I wept at the generosity of one who had nothing.

I think of the children here. The fact that they would prefer pen and paper to sweets. That they laugh and play as our children do back home when they have the security to do so. They exude hope. They are the future.

Hope. Not just a whimsical wish, but the belief and desire that things will turn out better than they are now.

This evening we celebrate the birth of the Christ child. God's message of hope for us all. A child born in poverty of a single mother becomes our salvation. It is in the birth of this child that our hope rests.

'And this shall be a sign unto you; Ye shall find the babe wrapped in swaddling clothes, lying in a manger. And suddenly there was with the angel a multitude of the heavenly host praising God, and saying, Glory to God in the highest, and on earth peace, good will toward men.'

May god bless you this Christmas and give you peace and hope.

Happy Christmas from Helmand

26 December 2009

Major Paul Smyth, RIFLES, Media Ops

This year, instead of waking up to two very excited little girls with stockings full of presents, I prised myself out of my winter sleeping bag and stepped out into a bitterly cold Christmas day in Helmand province, Afghanistan.

I have been in the reserves now for just over eight years and have spent lots of time away in places like Iraq and Kosovo, and I have been to Afghanistan once before. But this has been the first time I have spent Christmas out of the country, let alone away from my family.

In all that time, although far from home in some very challenging places, I know that it is harder for wives and children than it is for us soldiers. Christmas is such a special day and with the girls just four and nearly six they are very aware that daddy is not there to share it with them.

But I was with a small team of British soldiers at Patrol Base Talibjan near Musa Qaleh, and we were just 2km from what is called the FLET or Forward Line Enemy Troops. And it was to the FLET that we headed out to on Christmas Eve.

Major Paul Smyth taking a break with other members of the team as the operation gets under way.

The Brits I was with work alongside the Afghan National Army, sharing the same basic mud-walled compound. Each day they patrol the surrounding area talking to the locals,

meeting with the Afghan National Police and reassuring their rural community with a 'hearts and minds' campaign. But Christmas Eve was different. While I would have given anything to be back with the family, the lads and I had to keep those thoughts at the back of our minds.

As you slept tucked up in bed with snowflakes falling outside, we were already in the thick of a firefight with the Taliban. Christmas Eve was a different operation altogether, not just one of the usual patrols. We were there to intentionally probe the Taliban, to test their positions and to test their resolve. To ensure we had the upper hand we brought in support.

Once the Taliban took us on and tried to outflank us, we pushed out our Scimitar light tanks and the armoured Mastiffs broke cover. For what seemed like ages the air filled with the sound of gunfire and the sonic cracks as Taliban bullets whizzed past our heads.

As we pushed them back, an RAF Tornado flew in low, drowning out every noise in its wake, reinforcing how serious we were in our intent that day.

The team had been awesome. We pushed back the Taliban, swept through their compounds and captured a raft of components destined to make deadly IEDs, the improvised explosive devices that soldiers here fear more than anything else. But we didn't get them all. One of the vehicles got hit by an IED. Luckily no one was hurt, the armour did its thing. It does make you think that as infantry on foot we can go wherever we choose. But in a vehicle you can be channelled by the terrain and targeted.

Not until we marched back through the fields and over the hills, and once the heavy body armour and day sacks were off, did we start to think of home – wondering what our loved ones were up to – maybe sledging. Then deep in our own quiet thoughts, as the events of the day sank in, did we really start to miss them.

But, being British soldiers we crack on and move forward. There was much to do. The Taliban don't take Christmas off, so nor do the troops. But we can always squeeze in a bit of a celebration as nothing gets in the way of Christmas. Many of us had parcels from family with Santa hats and treats. We even had a small Christmas tree, not a real one, but it was there flashing away in the ops room.

A frozen turkey had arrived together with stuffing, carrots, potatoes and sprouts. And the Afghan soldiers' bread oven had inspired our ammo tin oven built into one of the compound walls that cooked the turkey to perfection.

With the sun blazing in the sky, I have to say I sat down to one of the most unusual Christmas lunches I think I will ever have. I pity the girls who will no doubt hear the tale each and every year as they grow older. But this year, using a satellite phone to talk to them, I told them Santa had visited the little boys and girls here, just like he had at home. For now they think that I am out here to help the little boys and girls have the sort of life that they take for granted. In a way that is what we are here to do. But for now, how we do that can wait, as they need not worry like my wife.

Hearing them laughing and giggling with excitement on the phone makes you realise how much you miss them. But, you have to stay strong and reassure them. However you feel at the time, it is not for them to hear, so that is not what they get.

With half of the tour complete, there is still a long way to go. Looking to the future I can see that I will be back here again. But, things are improving. The ANA we fought alongside are getting better all the time. Once we get them up to speed fully and they can master their own destiny, we and the International Security Assistance Force can come home.

What a day, what a Christmas Eve and what a way to celebrate Christmas. I know it isn't the norm but it is what we are trained for, it is what we expect. It is hard out here and the environment is tough, but we take pride in what we are doing and we will do the very best that we can.

Lying here, in the cold on my cot bed with what seems like all of my clothes on, there is just one thing left to say, and that's 'Happy Christmas' from Helmand. We're thinking of you.

Operation Spamalot

4 January 2010

Sergeant Bob Seely, Intelligence Corps (V), Media Ops

Most chefs have given up using spam in exchange for far more exotic ingredients, but after working up in Northern Helmand I found one Army chef, Corporal Liam Francis, who has proved it's a lifesaver serving troops on the front line.

A civilian supply chopper flying to forward operating bases (FOB) in Sangin, where Corporal Francis was based, had been

Corporal Liam Francis cooking in the main kitchen in Camp Bastion. [Picture: Cpl Steve Blake]

shot down by the Taliban, and no fresh food was coming in as a result. They were on compo (compound rations) for six weeks and amazingly they only had one menu: spam.

Not being put off, he put his ingenuity to the test and devised as many recipes as he could. He even surprised himself with what he could do: sweet and sour spam, spam fritters, spam carbonara, spam stroganoff, spam stir-fry ... to name but a few. His creations produced a series of dishes to rival the famous Monty Python Spam sketch.

Food is critical to soldiers. As the old saying goes, an Army marches on its stomach. It is also a critical morale booster for infantry troops, which patrol every day and are often in firefights with the Taliban.

A month and a half after Corporal Francis arrived, fresh food finally got to the base. The first day off spam he prepared battered sausages, chips and curry sauce. The sergeant major told him it was the best meal he had ever had – and that he'd never seen morale so high!

Luckily for the guys in Sangin district, the chopper flights are now far more regular and fresh food is getting in to most of the forward operating bases.

Soon after the 42 days of spam, Corporal Francis swapped the FOB for the UK's main base in Helmand province, Camp Bastion, where Army and civilian chefs turn out 12,000 meals a day for the troops based in and transiting through. The kitchens at Camp Bastion get through 7,500 burgers a week, 10 tonnes of chicken breast a month, 20,000 baguettes a week and 4.5 tonnes of potatoes and chips.

What 'success' will mean for us

8 January 2010

Lieutenant Colonel J.M.J. Bennett, Commanding Officer, 1 Royal Horse
Artillery (RHA) and Joint Fires & Intelligence, Surveillance,
Target Acquisition, and Reconnaissance (ISTAR) Group

As we approach the mid-point of the tour, it is worth reminding ourselves of what 'success' will mean for 11 Brigade and for the 1 Royal Horse Artillery based Joint Fires & ISTAR Group (JFIG). Overall, the brigade commander sees this tour as setting the campaign onto a firm, clear footing, making it easier for others to follow. This approach incorporates a number of areas. Firstly, the PRT-owned Helmand Plan sets out progress in each district towards Afghan autonomy of

Commanding Officer of 1st Regiment Royal Horse Artillery, Lieutenant Colonel J.M.J. Bennett.

governance, security, infrastructure, economic development, etc. This does not mean we are looking for the 'exit', but without articulating the end state and the means of delivering it, we cannot actually define success or be clear whether one is succeeding. Within the Helmand Plan, the military own the security line (shared between Task Force Helmand (TFH) and Task Force Leatherneck (TFL)).

The TFH Security Plan (the sum of a number of Battlegroup plans) envisages 'protected communities' with, ultimately, Afghan National Police (ANP) on the inside of the community, Afghan National Army (ANA) as an outer cordon, and ISAF protecting in depth. This is of course subject to police training and delivering embedded partnering (EbP). Ultimately, therefore, EbP with the ANA and ANP development will eventually enable the transition to Afghan National Security Forces (ANSF) primacy in Helmand. Of course, the enemy retain a vote in the meantime, hence we continue to push the Taliban further away from the population centres in order to make the overall plan easier to achieve. The brigade won't achieve all this before we leave in April, but we will have set the conditions for it all to happen.

Specifically within the JFIG, we have made much progress. It is worth reiterating just how good our training was in preparing us for the realities of operations in Afghanistan. Assisted by some really clear direction from COM ISAF, we were able to replicate in the UK the types of scenario we would find in theatre and refine our responses accordingly. In practice, this meant achieving a mind-set of NOT using force unless we needed to, rather than the traditional model of responding to force with more force. As a result, we continue to see reductions in the amount of lethal artillery and mortar ammunition fired, without seeing an increase in the number of UK military casualties. Indeed, the real benefit appears to be that the local people perceive a less noisy battlefield to mean a more secure environment, and therefore there are positive signs of closer relationships with the local people, something the Taliban find increasingly frustrating.

The JFIG continues to deliver a combination of force protection to our troops and precision targeting of the Taliban to assist the freedom of movement for both ourselves and the local population. Interestingly, of the artillery ammunition so far fired, over three-quarters of it has been non-lethal (smoke and illumination), designed to enable our troops to move unseen or work more effectively at night.

Firing a Light Gun.

The boys and girls on the gun lines split their time between firing the guns or rockets and protecting their bases, whilst getting enough time to do some exercise, phone home and even conduct some self-generated education! We also continue to develop the Afghan Artillery capability, and the relationship between the British instructors and Afghan students is increasingly like a partnership – the level of camaraderie and soldierly banter amongst them is great to see.

For the moment, we also have a team of Gunners working in the Helmand Police Training Centre (HPTC). Its first 150 Afghan Police recruits are undertaking a short course to develop their teamwork and policing skills within the complex, often violent environment of Helmand. Again, the degree of interaction between Brits and Afghans is impressive, with each understanding the psychology of the other increasingly well. The variety of our role has even extended to one of the Gunner captains taking temporary command of his infantry company whilst his boss is on leave in the UK. He has loved the opportunity and the company have continued to perform strongly.

◪ Royal Welsh target Taliban in their biggest assault yet

18 January 2010

Major Paul Smyth, RIFLES, Media Ops

More than 300 helicopter-borne soldiers have targeted a Taliban stronghold in one of their biggest operations since arriving in Helmand over a month ago. Soldiers from the 1st Battalion The Royal Welsh, newly arrived in, have been conducting air assault operations in an area known as The Babaji Pear because of its distinctive shape on the map.

The 'Pear' includes part of western Babaji, the area where fierce fighting took place last summer in Operation Panther's Claw, and the north-eastern Nad-e-Ali district.

Commanders hailed the assault as 'extremely successful', with no soldiers killed or wounded throughout.

The area where the assault took place is an insurgent stronghold and the troops have been building up to this Battlegroup operation with a series of smaller raids aimed at disrupting them. Codenamed Operation Bambirik, the Welsh soldiers worked alongside the Afghan National Army during the four-day mission, with the ANA making up a quarter of the force.

Three RAF Chinooks head into the Landing Zone from the east. RAF Merlins come in from the west and Army Air Corps Apache helicopters provide the protection. [Picture: Major Paul Smyth]

The young Afghan National Army platoon commander working alongside The Royal Welsh. [Picture: Major Paul Smyth]

We British see the Afghans' role as vital as they are far better at engaging with the locals who up until now have never seen the new Afghan soldiers in this part of Helmand. The operation was not without risk and the troops were engaged in numerous contacts involving small arms fire and rocket-propelled grenades. On several occasions insurgents used children as human shields and locals were herded into the open in an attempt to draw fire.

D Company, along with the commanding officer, flew into the area at last light, while the Mobility Reconnaissance Force with me tagging along, together with a platoon of Afghan National Army, supported them using a patrol base on the northern edge of The Pear as a staging area.

For the Royal Welsh, helicopters are providing them with the ability to get out on the ground. By flying into the heart of Taliban territory, the soldiers can avoid the lethal IEDs that surround the patrol bases and disrupt the insurgents where they least expect it.

How to get around in Helmand

20 January 2010

Tim, Economic Adviser, PRT

Since I joined the Helmand Provincial Reconstruction Team in November, I've seen some great progress being made here, but I've also seen the huge challenges involved in helping the Afghan people govern this country for themselves.

Just before Christmas, Douglas Alexander, the Secretary of State for International Development, visited Helmand and I travelled with him to Nad-e-Ali district, ten miles north-west of where I'm based in Lashkar Gah. We met Nad-e-Ali's District Governor – a friendly, committed and energetic man with a big beard, called Habibullah. He proudly showed off the local high school which was recently rebuilt, the community health centre which was closed under the Taliban but has now reopened, and the new road which has been laid through the bazaar – all with my team's support.

As we were walking along, Habibullah told me how he grew up in a nearby village and longed for things to return to the way they were before the fighting. He led us into a room full of 'white beards' – local elders who sit on the Community Council and help him to govern the district. Because of the decades of conflict here, many people have never had any contact with the Government. We're working with Habibullah to extend the reach of the Community Council so that people in Nad-e-Ali can access basic Government services and don't have to rely on the brutal justice of the Taliban.

The Council were busy agreeing next year's budget – a process which involves lengthy negotiations and lots of tea drinking – so we left them to it and wandered round the thriving bazaar where local farmers were selling fruit and vegetables. I was surprised by how safe – and how unlike a war zone – it all felt.

Habibullah lives in the District Centre in northern Nad-e-Ali, which was cleared by the British military during Operation Red Dagger early last year and is now relatively prosperous. The southern parts of the district remain under Taliban control though, and outside of the District Centre things look very different. Because of the security situation we had to travel there by helicopter. It's exciting running up the ramp onto a Chinook while the rotors are still turning – but the difficulty of travelling across Helmand makes reconstruction and development much harder. Whether local businesses are trying to transport their goods to market or Government officials are trying to visit the districts they govern, freedom of movement is critical.

My team works closely with the Provincial Government and the UK and US military to improve security and increase freedom of movement in Helmand. For example, we've helped to lay around 100km of hard-surface roads across the province. Hard-surface roads are easier to travel on. They're also harder to bury an IED under. Steps like these help

Habibullah and other Helmandis to get on with their daily lives without fear of being attacked by the Taliban. Across the country, work is also being done to clear landmines left over from previous conflicts. But progress can be slow, and rebuilding Afghanistan will take both time and commitment.

I'm now busy preparing for the International Afghanistan Conference in London later this month. The aim of the conference is to raise more support for the Government of Afghanistan to deliver security and improve economic development across the country.

◤ A challenging three months

25 January 2010

Lieutenant Colonel Harry Fullerton, Commanding Officer,

The Household Cavalry Regiment Battlegroup

For the last three months, The Household Cavalry Regiment (HCR) has been deployed in three distinct groups in Helmand province.

Making up a considerable part of Battlegroup North West, which controls the Musa Qaleh area of Task Force Helmand, is the Battlegroup Headquarters, Headquarter Squadron and C Squadron, plus an Armoured Infantry Company of A Company, 2nd Battalion The Royal Welsh, B Company, 2nd Battalion The Yorkshire Regiment (2 YORKS), and A Company, 1st Battalion The Royal Anglians.

The next group, which is further afield and away from the Battlegroup, is A Squadron, who have been based in both Camp Bastion and FOB Price and have found themselves working in the Babaji area.

The third group is B Squadron, which is the Brigade Reconnaissance (Recce) Force, which has been tasked across the whole area, but has mostly been deployed in the central area of Helmand.

These first three months have been challenging, but a great deal of success has been achieved during this time and the Battlegroup and our detached squadrons feel confident of doing more to ensure the security of the people of Helmand, to defeat the insurgency, and to partner and train up the Afghan security forces.

We had an excellent handover from 2nd Battalion The Royal Regiment of Fusiliers, giving us enough knowledge and insight of the area that we could maintain the tempo of operations in Musa Qaleh.

Musa Qaleh has been an area of increasing stability and security over the past 12 months, with the area under control of the Government growing on a regular basis. Such is the confidence of the local people that there is a bustling bazaar area and two large markets that occur each week in the wadi [dry river bed], and all this is done without the need for any overt military security presence.

From left to right: Major Tom Barker, Captain Brian Rogers, Major Rob Philipson-Stow, Lieutenant Colonel Harry Fullerton, Captain Matt Nichol, Captain Nick Van-Cutsen and Warrant Officer Class 1 Aide Gardner. [Picture: Sgt Rob Knight]

The powerhouse for the troops, the cookhouse at Musa Qaleh. [Picture: Sgt Rob Knight]

The key theme of the tour has been about working with our Afghan partners, both the Police and Army. The Afghan Police have recently been on an intense training programme, run by the Americans. The finished product is a District Police Force that are better trained and disciplined and who are now gaining the respect of the locals, something that was perhaps missing in the past.

The development of the police is vital to the long-term stability of Musa Qaleh and we are heading in the right direction. The Afghan Army battalion (called a Kandak) in Musa Qaleh is a professional body, commanded by an experienced commanding officer who has thorough knowledge of the area.

The Kandak has recently been reinforced with new soldiers, increasing its strength by nearly a Company's worth. What we have been doing is working ever more closely with the Afghan Army and Police.

In addition to the Kandak's Companies that are mentored by B Company, 2nd Battalion The Yorkshire Regiment, we are also planning our operations jointly at Battlegroup and Company level and then executing these plans in a partnered manner. ISAF and Afghan forces complement each other with different specialist skills and we have discovered how good the Afghans are at reading the ground and clearing through built-up areas.

Together we are achieving more. The recent villages reclaimed in the south were a prime example of this co-operation.

I expect that the next few months will see an ever more confident community, an expanding area of Government control and further moves on our part to partner with the Afghan National Security Forces.

The other possibility is that I would hope to see some moves by the less motivated insurgents to down tools and attempt reintegration with the community. We have already seen the beginnings of this and we hope for more.

Last but not least, Musa Qaleh is about to see some significant reconstruction and development, with a new mosque being built in the centre of town, new Government offices, a causeway being built across the wadi, and a route improvement being planned in the direction of Gereshk. We should also see the completion of the new police station. All in all, there is a great deal of investment going into the town.

At the smaller scale, there have been many projects to build and open schools, repair roads, drill for water holes and teach people basic construction skills.

There is no doubt that Musa Qaleh is a thriving town with great potential in the near future. The ANSF are strong and are improving all the time. Security is improving and the people are becoming more confident in the ability of the Afghan Government to deliver the security and services that they need.

◱ Birth of the Afghan Army is the British exit strategy

26 January 2010

Lieutenant Sally Armstrong, RN

With the end of my tour looming, I wanted to go beyond the Helmand-centric view of the campaign and look at the work being done by Brits elsewhere in Afghanistan. So, in the mountainous outskirts of the Afghan capital, on a vast exercise area littered with rusting Soviet-era tanks and derelict buildings, British infantry commander Lieutenant Colonel Nick Ilic explains to me why training the Afghan National Army is crucial to British success in Afghanistan: 'It is absolutely fundamental we get this right. This is our exit strategy. The guys down south in Helmand and elsewhere are holding the line, creating a safe environment for us to train the Afghan National Army to the right standard and quality so they can take on the fight when they're ready.'

British, American and other NATO soldiers are working together to train and mentor thousands of ANA soldiers each month at the flagship Military Training Centre, Kabul (KMTC).

Lieutenant Colonel Ilic, 41, a father of six from Warminster in Wiltshire, is the UK Leadership Training Team's (LTT's) commanding officer, based at Camp Alamo, near KMTC. He heads up a team of 64 British military personnel charged with overseeing the ANA's Officer and Senior Non-Commissioned Officer (SNCO) training. The training of junior ANA soldiers is run by US military teams.

Lieutenant Colonel Nick Ilic out on the training area with an Afghan. [Picture: Lt Sally Armstrong]

In the past, ANA training was delivered by coalition forces, but now, Lieutenant Colonel Ilic explains it is delivered by the ANA themselves: 'My team advises, mentors and trains the ANA instructors who run the training. The aim is for Afghans to lead the training of other Afghans; when required to do so we step in and assist in the training ourselves. The mentors are here to ensure that the training is carried out safely and that standards are kept high.

Warriors at the flagship Military Training Centre, Kabul. [Picture: Lt Sally Armstrong]

'Witnessing the birth of this new Afghan Army is a humbling experience. There is no doubting the enthusiasm of the troops. They're all determined to make a better Afghanistan for themselves and their families. The fact they are joining in their droves illustrates there's a newfound confidence in Afghanistan.'

The ANA trainee soldiers at KMTC are recruited from all over Afghanistan. They pass through an eight-week training package of basic infantry and core military skills essential for fighting the Taliban – such as weapon handling, live firing, section attacks and compound clearances – before graduating and deploying to the various provinces in ethnically mixed teams.

Some deploy to live and fight alongside British soldiers in Operational Mentoring and Liaison Teams (OMLTs) in Helmand province's Green Zone, where fierce fighting with insurgents takes place. Others deploy to work alongside units like the 1st Battalion The Royal Welsh who are partnered with ANA soldiers, and over the course of the next three months, numbers will grow until an entire Kandak (the equivalent of a British battalion) will live and fight alongside the Welsh soldiers.

The mentoring staff at Alamo are responsible for ensuring the ANA is trained to a strength of 134,000 by the end of October 2010. Initially, the Army will be an infantry centric force able to fight insurgents and hold the ground until the national force reaches full operational capability – with its own logistic and support elements – of 171,600 by the end of October 2011.

Lieutenant Colonel Ilic is under no illusions about the size of the task ahead, but is infectiously optimistic about the prospect of success: 'To reach that target we need to train 5,200 soldiers, officers and NCOs every month and we've already trained 100,000 – that's a similar number to the total size of the British Army. At the moment recruiting is high because the harvests are in and people are looking for other employment. The challenge is to maintain that momentum in spring and summer, but we're confident we'll be able to achieve that.'

Recruitment has undoubtedly been assisted by the doubling of salaries. A Warrior fighting in Helmand (the equivalent rank to a British private soldier) now receives $240 per month – an attractive prospect when over half the Afghan population lives below the poverty line. In a move to prevent corruption, the money is paid into the soldiers' own private bank accounts rather than as cash.

'Managing the training is a huge challenge and resources are probably the biggest challenge. We are bulging at the seams here at KMTC. To cope, we are expanding the training bases so that training Afghans can take place in each of the regional core areas of Gardez, Herat, Kandahar and Maz i Sharif.'

Lieutenant Colonel Ilic refutes allegations that the quantity of ANA soldiers being trained is trumping quality: 'The training at KMTC is only the first leg in a relay race. After graduating, the soldiers undertake selection and training for specialist roles followed by pre-deployment training and then partnering on the front line by embedded training and mentoring teams. KMTC is therefore the start of a long training cycle that each ANA soldier must undertake to ensure an army of the right quality and size is developed to guarantee the long-term stability and future of Afghanistan.'

Literacy is also a key area that the British team are addressing. Every recruit receives a two-week literacy course when they join. At each and every stage of training after that, such as the NCO courses, they undertake a further week's literacy training. This is invaluable as reading and writing are skills for life and the soldiers are very aware of the value this brings them.

The British have been training and mentoring their Afghan counterparts since 2006 and are constantly developing the training programmes to make sure they are efficient and relevant to the current operational environment. Drill, for example, has been reduced to make room for more weapons training.

From June, different specialist schools will begin to be established, with the British leading on the delivery of Combat Arms skills such as infantry and artillery training.

'We are not trying to create a British Army – ours has been hundreds of years in the making. What the ANA needs to be able to do is to take on and defeat the Taliban. They can achieve that because they are better trained, better equipped and better motivated with a long-term future. In time, quantity and quality will tell.'

Lieutenant Colonel Ilic has been personally mentoring Colonel Abdul Sabor, the ANA Non-Commissioned Officers' Academy Commander. Colonel Sabor says the relationship between the mentors and the ANA is good: 'We have one aim, one enemy. The ANA is improving all the time and after four or five years, with the help of coalition forces, there'll be no al-Qaida or Taliban in Afghanistan.'

◣ Behind the headlines, what is it like to fight in Afghanistan?

27 January 2010

Major Richard Streatfield, Officer Commanding A Company, 4 RIFLES

It's a paradox. Having achieved relative control of our new area the fight is now on to keep control.

The insurgent is tenacious as well as brutal. We treated a local who had stepped on and partially detonated a roadside bomb. He was flown by us to the hospital in Lashkar Gah.

During his stay there, his family came to the patrol base where he had been treated to see if we had any news. As they departed they were followed. We found out that the insurgent intended to question them and stop them ever talking to us again. The unveiled threat of the bully. We paid for his father to take a taxi to the hospital.

Our man now is back, down a foot unfortunately, but extremely grateful for his treatment and speedy evacuation.

The platoon commander who organised the evacuation is now a family friend. An invitation to supper has been extended.

Of particular interest to the Afghans is the presence of a female medic. She provokes confusion and admiration in equal measure.

In this conflict the front line is not a line in the dust. It is waged over the human geography. It is politics with an admixture of other means; the battle for trust and support over coercion.

However, in Afghanistan people trust what they can see. The presence of a patrol base may bring explosions and fighting but people feel safer.

The greatest paradox of all is that in our area, as the casualties in the security cordon continue, the centre of Sangin is as safe and prosperous as it has ever been.

⬛ Wishtan – the Devil's playground

29 January 2010

Major Graeme Wearmouth, B Company, The Royal Scots Borderers

Each patch in Helmand presents a different challenge to operate in. Certain places earn reputations more chilling than others. In the summer of 2009, Wishtan in East Sangin earned such a reputation. The sacrifices made by the Company from 2nd Battalion The Rifles based in Wishtan during that time are sadly well known, and recognition for their heroism well deserved. We picked up their baton, and halfway through our own tour it is worth reflecting on what has been achieved since September.

Outwardly not much is different. Our manning, equipment, general tactics and approach are similar. There have inevitably been tactical developments allowing us to target the IED layers with more success. We are wary of tempting fate, and our unofficial mottoes have become 'a day at a time' and 'you are only as good as your next patrol'.

We have a long way to go on this tour and it remains a deadly battle. The margin for error is slim but we have built on the work of our predecessors, and the words of their outgoing commanders urging us to take this place forward still feel like a big responsibility – but one that we will shoulder.

The daily reminder to do our duty is the cross bearing the names of those who have fallen here before. Our path has, as you would expect, not been easy. We have had our own wounds to see to. But we have also had success.

Our success may seem gradual to the West, but the significance of steps like successfully encouraging locals to use roads and compounds they previously have not, whether due to IEDs or a misplaced fear of soldiers, cannot be underestimated.

Locals are now more willing to come forward and speak to us, cautiously at first but with more confidence day by day.

They have seen the time-consuming and high-risk clearance operations we have carried out to ensure their roads and compounds are safe. Their hopes are very similar to our own – security, prosperity and a better life for their children.

B Company, The Royal Scots Borderers at Wishtan. [Picture: Lt Sally Armstrong]

Most of the Afghans who remain in Wishtan's high-walled compounds are wonderfully hospitable and show real understanding for the campaign that is being fought around them. Yes, they may sit on the fence due to fear of insurgent backlash, waiting to see who endures as the dominating force – but they do not enjoy the oppression the insurgency brings.

We speak to the victims of the insurgency – the fathers whose children have been killed by IEDs while playing in the street, and the already impoverished who have their money and supplies stolen from them. These people understandably plead for revenge.

Polishing the brass plates on the Wishtan Memorial. [Picture: Lt Sally Armstrong]

There have been isolated examples of insurgents rejected by the locals, but we want to see this trickle become a steady stream and then a surge. That is the longer-term hope, and as the Afghan Security Forces develop, the people's confidence to stand up will follow. In the meantime, they quietly tell us about dangers and about the methods of intimidation they face. They attend Shuras and quietly accept grants from the Government to develop their communities, which are real signs of progress.

I will not claim that we have turned the corner in four months. This is a long campaign and we know from bitter experience that the insurgents have not disappeared. They have kept up their activity over the colder months but have been unable to halt the development work being done. This is a sign of the growing will of the local people and we hope it will continue.

⬃ Another day, another bomb

2 February 2010

Sergeant Bob Seely, Intelligence Corps (V), Media Ops

At Patrol Base Talibjan in the rocky Afghan desert, a couple of kilometres from Taliban insurgent positions, Staff Sergeant Gareth Wood walks towards a mark on the ground under which 20kg of ammonium nitrate and aluminium, the ingredients of a powerful improvised bomb, are hidden.

Staff Sergeant
Gareth Wood.

His colleagues wait behind hard cover as he lies in front of the device. Wood quietly goes through his drills. For ten minutes he works inches from the bomb, identifies the components and, using his fingers to feel the device, disarms it. Job done, he calmly walks back to re-join his colleagues. He tells me it's all about keeping your cool. You can't rush things, no matter what the threat out there is.

The Royal Logistic Corps' Explosive Ordnance Disposal teams and the Royal Engineers' search teams, responsible between them for finding, isolating and defusing the lethal bombs designed to destroy men and machinery, are fast becoming the heroes of Britain and NATO's Afghanistan counter-insurgency campaign. Soldiers ranging from privates to commanding officers have no doubt that these remarkable men and women are saving many lives.

As the day progressed, more IEDs around the base and on the main road, a dirt track nearby, were found – eight in total. From 10 a.m. through to mid-afternoon the sound of thumps echoed throughout the Talibjan Valley as Staff Sergeant Wood's team, supported by three US colleagues, safely detonated the detected devices.

UK troops defeat the enemy in open combat, so Taliban guerrillas have resorted to paying or coercing others to plant explosives for them, including children, as a way of generating headlines and harming UK troops.

In response, the Army has set up a Counter-IED Task Force to study the Taliban's methods and develop new tactics and equipment, much of it secret, to find and destroy the bombs before they explode. In addition, infantry soldiers are becoming increasingly skilled in identifying IEDs, thanks to new training and equipment.

Wood remarks that the Counter-IED Task Force is important to the war. Their work finding and disposing of IEDs allows the Battlegroups to maintain their freedom of movement and also allows Afghan civilians to go about their daily lives. Indeed, many of the victims of the IED war are poor Afghan farmers or children, who pick up the detonators thinking that they are toys, only to have hands and feet blown off.

For Wood it's cowardly the way they are fighting. It's very indiscriminate the amount of casualties caused to Afghan children. Such is the backlash from locals that British soldiers in the Musa Qaleh area are seeing many more 'walk-ins' from Afghans fed up with the Taliban's tactics.

Although some do detonate, a large percentage of bombs are found and made safe. In addition, heavily armoured new vehicles such as Mastiffs mean that soldiers are increasingly likely to survive bomb blasts should they occur. It takes years of painstaking training to reach the top of the bomb disposal team. Staff Sergeant Wood has had six years' experience to reach the level of High Threat IEDD (Improvised Explosive Device Disposal) Operator. Luckily, today there was no firing from the enemy, although sometimes Wood and his team have to work under small arms fire.

◥ Operation Moshtarak

11 February 2010
Brigadier James Cowan, Commander Task Force Helmand,
11 Light Brigade

We stand here today as partners. In the past few weeks we have trained to be a combined force. Soon we will be part of an operation, the like of which has not been seen since the start of this campaign: Operation Moshtarak, or in English, 'Together'.

I can think of no better name to describe this venture. For we are in this together: we have planned it together, we will fight it together, we will see it through together.

Afghans with Allies, soldiers with civilians, Government with its people.

Brigadier James Cowan and General Mohaiyodin, Commander of 3rd Brigade, 205 Corps, of the Afghan National Army, address troops before Operation Moshtarak begins. [Picture: Staff Sgt Will Craig]

In the last few weeks we have seized the initiative from the enemy. Day after day for six weeks we have killed and captured the enemy's leaders, shaping the conditions for success. Soon we will clear the Taliban from its safe havens in central Helmand. Where we go, we will stay. Where we stay, we will build.

We will establish security so that the people are free once more to live their own lives under their own Government.

The next few days will not be without danger. To reduce the risks you must know your enemy. Avoid the places they would expect you to go. Stay off the tracks. Check vulnerable areas before you enter them. Watch out for propaganda traps. Be first with the truth.

Above all else, protect the people. Defeat the enemy by avoiding civilian casualties. Hold your fire if there is risk to the innocent, even if this puts you in greater danger. That kind of restraint requires courage. The courageous restraint you have shown throughout our time in Afghanistan.

Offer an open hand in friendship to those who do not wish to fight. They can join the people of Afghanistan and their Government in rebuilding their society.

For those who will not shake our hand they will find it closed into a fist. They will be defeated.

With my Afghan friends, I am proud to be one of your commanders. Together, Operation Moshtarak will mark the start of the end of the insurgency. I wish you Godspeed and the best of luck.

◥ The clearance phase

13 February 2010

Major Paul Smyth, RIFLES, Media Ops

On Saturday 13 February the key military 'clearing' phase of Operation Moshtarak, involving a combined force of 15,000 troops launching major assaults on Taliban strongholds, started in central Helmand province.

The operations are designed to clear the region of insurgents and set the conditions for the Government of Afghanistan to introduce increased security, stability, development, rule of law, freedom of movement and reconstruction.

Op Moshtarak focuses on the area of Marjah, with operations being led by Afghan forces and US Marines, and Nad-e-Ali, where Afghan, British, Canadian and other American forces lead the attack.

This is the first part of a three-stage plan to increase security in the country. After the insurgency in the south has been subdued, British forces will move to building capacity in the

Soldiers from 1st Battalion The Royal Welsh get ready for the start of Operation Moshtarak. [Picture: Staff Sgt Will Craig]

Afghan National Security Forces and this will likely become the main effort later in the year.

The third stage will be transition and the reintegration of insurgents and sympathisers into Afghan society through an Afghan-led reintegration policy.

This combined force includes:

• Approximately five brigades of Afghan forces, including members of the Afghan National Army, Afghan National Police, Afghan Border Police and the Afghan National Civil Order Police.

• ISAF Regional Command (South) elements, with forces drawn from the United States, the United Kingdom, Denmark, Estonia and Canada.

◪ A scene that I have never experienced before

13 February 2010

Lieutenant Colonel Rosie Stone, Adjutant General's Corps (V),

Media Ops

Lights from my vehicle briefly lit up a line of tense faces as I passed column after column of British and Afghan soldiers, interspersed with French and Estonians, en route to the helicopter flight line at Camp Bastion. It was 3 o'clock in the morning and finally, after weeks of training and preparation, Op Moshtarak was officially under way.

The heavy sound of dozens of rotor blades turning filled the air, and dust kicked up by all the activity hit the back of my throat as I stepped out onto one of the forming-up points.

My team's job was to ensure that all the embedded journalists who will be covering the operation from the front line were delivered to the right helicopter on time. It marked the end of the busiest 48 hours the Joint Media Operations Centre has experienced since the start of 11 Light Brigade's tour in Helmand province.

As with the Battlegroup soldiers and aircrew gathered throughout Bastion, we had experienced laughter, nerves and a sense of camaraderie with our media guests, but now everyone was firmly focused on the job ahead.

Large groups of men moved into their pre-allotted holding areas. Some carried ladders over their shoulders, ready to be used for climbing over the walls into village compounds. Others were burdened with the powerful general purpose machine gun and heavy belts of ammunition. Corporal Lino Woolfe from the Royal Army Veterinary Corps quietly knelt beside his specialist search dog, patiently waiting to be loaded onto his assigned Merlin helicopter.

Soldiers from 1st Battalion The Royal Welsh get ready to be lifted by helicopter at the start of the operation. [Picture: Staff Sgt Will Craig]

It was a scene that I have never experienced before in the twenty-two years that I have served in the military and will likely never experience again. The mix of tension and anticipation was tangible from the Battlegroup.

At the designated time loadmasters signalled for the groups to move, and in a well-practised drill hundreds of troops shouldered their kit and marched in single lines up the helicopter ramps and disappeared from view.

I then moved round to the end of the runway and witnessed a historic sight as wave after wave of helicopters rose up from the dust and the darkness, heading north-east towards Nad-e-Ali.

My enduring memory will be looking up into the sky as the lines of helicopters gradually faded into the distance looking like a string of pale amber fairy lights.

⬉ Morning airborne assault

14 February 2010

Flight Lieutenant Chris 'Haz' Hasley, RAF

After an in-depth planning and briefing process my crew and I walked to our Chinook for the morning assault. We had known about Op Moshtarak since our arrival in theatre back in December and as we loaded our troops and engaged the rotors, we were acutely aware of the complexity of the operation we were about to execute.

With eight minutes to go to launch, I noticed a splattering of oil accumulating on the windscreen. We consulted our ground crew who advised us to shut down the aircraft so that they could climb on top for a closer look. After a short interval, which seemed like a lifetime, they told us that there was a leak from one of our rotor blade nods but that the Chinook was safe to fly. With that information we set about restarting the cab as quickly as possible; a process that normally takes 15 minutes. We were airborne and in formation in less than five minutes, overall a minute later than planned.

We struck out at low level under the moonless night towards our objective, which was the insurgent-held town of Showal. En route to target, the ambient light levels were so poor that even our Night Vision Goggles (NVGs) struggled to provide much more than a dark-green nothingness.

On short finals to the target, the formation of Chinooks tightened spacing and pitched noses up hard to decelerate quickly. The back wheels dug into the soft ground of the muddy field and we disgorged our complement of Royal Welsh and ANA troops. Seconds later we were wheels up and racing back to Bastion airfield to pick up our next chalk of soldiers.

In just over 2 hours our packet of 4 RAF Chinooks had delivered approximately 650 soldiers to the heart of the insurgency. An insurgency who, after being forewarned of our attack, wisely kept their heads down or fled the scene.

Flight Lieutenant 'Haz' Hasley in the cockpit of his Chinook.

At 0610 we stopped the rotors and after a quick debrief headed for bed. We wouldn't get much sleep as we were taking over the Immediate Response Team helicopter later that day.

⌁ Staring down Taliban spotters

15 February 2010

Sergeant Major Sean Semple, Royal Engineers

We're off. We've got the nod from the commanding officer that Operation Moshtarak is finally happening. I can tell you the lads are relieved. We've been planning this for a long time. And the sooner we start, the sooner we finish.

The younger guys – those who've never heard an eve of battle address – are excited. The older ones amongst us, we're more pensive. We've been here before.

1 Looking north towards Musa Qaleh in Northern Helmand, home to The Household Cavalry
Regiment Battlegroup. *All images courtesy of Major Paul Smyth*

2 A 105mm Light Gun marks the two minutes' silence on Remembrance Day.

3 A silhouette of an RAF Merlin helicopter. After ten days of operational flying the helicopters have reached initial operating capability a month earlier than expected.

4 An Afghan shepherd at one of the regular clinics held by vet Captain Miles Malone.

5 At US$70 a piece, sheep are prized possessions, especially when a rural wage can be a dollar a day.

6 Heading back to Camp Bastion from Northern Helmand after the first operational sortie for the Merlin in Afghanistan.

7 In December the Duke of York makes a surprise visit to Helmand. During the trip he meets Lieutenant Commander Bill O'Brien, a fellow Falklands War veteran who won the Distinguished Flying Medal (DFM) during the conflict in the South Atlantic.

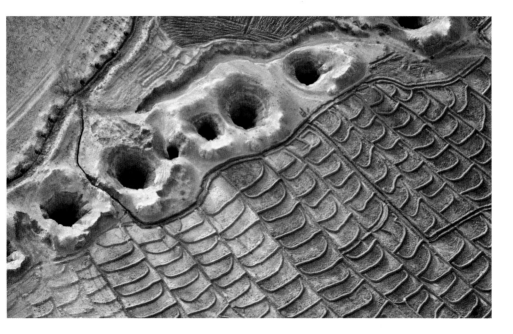

8 Farming has had a big impact on Helmand. These giant water boreholes are used to pump water into the complex irrigation systems.

9 On route from Musa Qaleh to Patrol Base Talibjan with the Afghan National Army (ANA) at the back of the convoy.

10 A very early and cold start to an operation, with the soldiers from 2 YORKS at Patrol Base Talibjan and their Afghan partners.

11 As the operation south of Patrol Base Talibjan gets under way, The Household Cavalry Regiment Scimitar armoured fighting vehicles move into place.

12 The Household Cavalry Regiment Scimitar armoured fighting vehicles break cover as the troops advance.

13 Heading back to Patrol Base Talibjan after a successful operation. The insurgent compounds have been cleared, a number of IEDs found and the Taliban have been left in no doubt as to who has the upper hand.

14 A well-earned communal meal after the operation. The kitchen at Talibjan is basic to say the least and consists of a wooden frame with plastic sheeting to keep out the elements. However, the food served up is great.

15 Sergeant Robinson (front left) with fellow troops at Talibjan.

16 Soldiers like those of Patrol Base Talibjan make what they can of Christmas Day in between patrols and compound clearances.

17 Corporal Graham Dransfield uses an Afghan-inspired oven to cook the turkey for Christmas Day.

18 Children always come out to watch patrols go by, but in the build-up to Operation Moshtarak, it is also the first time people from the area known as The Babaji Pear – because of its distinctive shape on the map – have seen the Afghan National Army.

19 The only females you will see on patrols in rural areas are the children, who often wear amazingly decorated clothing.

20 There is never any shortage of children eager for the boiled sweets that come in our ration packs.

21 Out with 1st Battalion The Royal Welsh on shaping operations before Operation Moshtarak.

22 Major Ed Hill alongside the ANA commander talking to locals in Nad-e-Ali district.

23 'Contact, wait out.' Major Ed Hill relays information back to HQ that the ANA troops with him have come under fire.

24 Moments before this picture is taken, Fusilier George Fisher was alongside the ANA in a firefight outside the compound.

25 Snipers keep tabs on the Taliban, who on several occasions are seen to use children as human shields and herd locals into the open in an attempt to draw fire.

26 Major Paul Smyth on Operation Bambirik with the 1st Battalion The Royal Welsh.

27 Rehearsals for Operation Moshtarak. Six different nations are taking part in the operation so practice is important.

28 Welsh and Afghan soldiers practise heli-drills before Operation Moshtarak.

29 To mark St David's Day, a lamb stew is delivered by one of the routine helicopter flights to the patrol base in the heart of Nad-e-Ali. It makes a very welcome change from the usual rations.

30 St David's Day rugby against French Foreign Legion soldiers working with The Royal Welsh.

31 The start of a typical patrol from Patrol Base Shaheed (2.5km north-east of Showal). The first job is to pick up some Afghan National Police from the local police checkpoint.

32 Afghan boys tend to the fields as the patrol heads by.

33 The Afghan National Army patrol commander gets ready to move off after a Shura with local farmers.

34 Moments after the patrol moves off, the Taliban open fire. The Welsh soldiers are at the rear of the patrol and make it no more than 15m from this point along the tree line before contact starts.

35 Lieutenant Adam Libby from B Company, 1 Royal Welsh, formulates a plan with the ANA commander and calls in air support.

36 The ANA patrol commander engages the insurgents.

7 A US fast jet comes in very low dropping flares in a 'show of force'. A demonstration of power like this is more than enough to put off the Taliban.

8 A typical Afghan kid that we pass on the way back to the patrol base after the firefight.

39 A French Foreign Legion soldier, part of the team helping to mentor the Afghans.

40 The distinctive shoulder flash of the French Foreign Legion.

41 A Royal Welsh Fusilier is weighed down by a mountain of kit taken out on a typical patrol.

42 Job done and heading back to the patrol base as the sun sets.

43 Fusilier Davis of the Quick Reaction Force (QRF) waits for the call. Every location has a QRF in case anything unexpected happens.

44 If the call comes in, the QRF will be good to go in minutes. They just need to grab their kit: helmet, body amour, weapons and day sacks.

45 The patrol base is up and running 24/7 with the Ops Room as its nerve centre.

46 Living on a diet of 24-hour ration packs is the norm out in the patrol bases. But when the guys can get hold of different ingredients, the 'Jamie Oliver' comes out in a handful of the lads and the results can be amazing.

47 Patrol base living is not for the faint-hearted. This is a typical ablution pulled together by the Engineers.

48 Getting to know the locals is vital, so the Welsh soldiers join the ANA and the Police to reassure the locals that things are getting better in this part of Helmand.

49 The Shura draws in a diverse range of locals from the area, keen to find out what the ISAF forces are planning.

50 Elders represent the villagers at the Shura.

51 Wherever I go with my camera it is like being the pied-piper. Everyone, especially the children, love seeing themselves on the monitor on the back of my digital camera. For most it is the first time they have seen their picture.

52 Not everyone is amused by the camera to start off with. However, it isn't long before this budding farmer who has come to see the vet is smiling.

53 The RAF Chinook is the workhorse of the helicopter fleet and the conditions in Helmand make using them extremely challenging.

54 Looking forward along a Chinook fuselage at the tapestry of fields that make up the Green Zone that follows the Helmand River.

55 HRH Prince Charles, The Prince of Wales, makes a surprise visit to Task Force Helmand Headquarters at Lashkar Gah to meet the troops and receive a brief from Brigadier James Cowan.

56 HRH Prince Charles is the most senior member of the royal family to visit Afghanistan and the only one in living memory to visit Kabul.

57 One of the most amazing sunsets I have ever seen. Helmand is a stunning place and I am constantly amazed by all the beautiful places I visit.

It's not fear of death – to be perfectly honest, I have total confidence in the vehicles – it's the unknown. You're prepared, but you don't know what to expect.

As we climbed into our Viking and Engineer vehicles we heard the helicopters go in. In my mind, I wish the guys well.

We left in the dark, but as our convoy rolled out you could feel the ground shuddering as we left. As sunlight broke over the desert, the scale of convoy took my breath away, nearly a mile long – that's the stuff that gives you confidence to deal with what's in front of you.

We stopped on the edge of the Green Zone – that's the fertile, agricultural bit of Helmand province where the enemy does most of their fighting. We prepare our leaguer – 24 Vikings Armoured Personnel Carriers (APC) arranged in a square like a metal fortress, with the Engineer's kit in the middle.

After lunch, I'm in a column that moves into Showal, the self-proclaimed 'capital' of the Taliban. It was a long, tense day – the enemy didn't stick around, they were running. We didn't see them. But we saw their IEDs.

At 2 p.m. we made a little bit of military history. We tried out a new piece of kit – the plough on the front of the Trojan – a converted Challenger 2.

The Trojan has other great bits on it too, including a rocket that fires a hose of a tonne and a half of high explosives to clear minefields. We didn't use that today, but we may do soon.

Plough leading, we drove down the middle of the wadi – dry river bed – punching through the IED belt.

The Engineers love their kit and they were in seventh heaven. Especially the commanding officer, Lieutenant Colonel Matt Bazeley. He's the guy who has been making sure this new stuff has got to theatre, and making sure it works. All credit to him. This stuff is going to save lives.

As for Showal, it was a ramshackle shanty town. How that can be the heart of anyone's world was beyond me. An eerie, empty place. All you could see was debris, open doorways, like something out of a spaghetti Western.

We walked only in the ground cleared by our plough and our Barma teams – those are the guys who risk life and limb day in day out to check the ground for IEDs.

As I look around at the desolate town, I saw, dead in front of me, a command wire. It caught my attention big style. No matter how many times people tell you about IEDS, when you see one yourself, it makes you think.

We found a couple of locals who hadn't fled. They told us: don't go past the two tyres laid on the road. It marks the line of safety: anything beyond may have IEDS under foot. Nasty cowards, the Taliban, I thought. They run away, but seeded their own town with mines.

After dark, we returned to the leaguer. We're out in the middle of nowhere – can't say exactly where – and surrounded by potential enemy, but you feel secure inside. Sentries cover all the angles.

We're all tired, it's been a long day. Now, it's no white light, minimal noise, heads down.

I climb into my sleeping bag, helmet and body armour next to me just in case.

Job done. Let's see what tomorrow brings.

↘ Combat medic

15 February 2010

Corporal Lucy Marrow, Combat Medical Technician

I normally train US soldiers in battlefield first aid but we've been building up for Op Moshtarak for a few days now, thoroughly checking our medical kits and the equipment in the vehicle. I've been training the Gurkha soldiers from the Logistics Regiment here in Camp Bastion as they load up all the supplies ready for the next phase of the operation. Now all the excitement of the helicopter drops is over, it is up to these guys on the ground to keep the momentum going.

It has given me the chance to work in Accident & Emergency at the Camp Bastion hospital, working on casualties and practising my clinical skills. We don't normally do this but my Squadron took the opportunity to filter us through the hospital to gain additional experience.

Corporal Lucy Marrow, Combat Medical Technician.

I've been out on several Combat Logistic Patrols, working from a Mastiff ambulance that can carry one stretcher casualty. It's the same as any other Mastiff out here, but inside it is fitted out like a Battlefield Ambulance – so it can carry oxygen and has places for all our medical equipment. I used to be apprehensive when I went out, but the Mastiff is a tough vehicle and I have already survived one IED strike where the Mastiff was slightly damaged but my team walked away without a scratch!

The Gurkhas are great guys. Being a girl they really look after me – if I need the toilet they will clear a path out to some cover for me so I can have some privacy. Other than that I'm treated pretty much like the lads.

Everyone is ready to go out there and support what the Royal Welsh and Afghan soldiers have achieved so far. Word is that the first two days have been easier than expected, but they will need more rations and other vital supplies to keep going, so we have been given notice to be ready to move any time from now.

The burden of responsibility

15 February 2010

Major Richard Gregory, Officer Commanding Fire Support Company, 1 Royal Welsh

I have never felt the burden of responsibility the way I did when we came in on this Operation. Not in Northern Ireland, nor in Iraq. Things went smoothly at Camp Bastion getting the guys loaded up and onto the helicopters. It was very tense flying into the landing zones but we were pleased to get out on the ground with very little drama.

Heavy mud in the fields made the going tough, but when we had made it safely in to our compound after being up to our knees in the mud in the dark, I thought – we have got it right. The patrol base is now established, however the hard work is still to be done. We now have to prove ourselves to the local

population and show them that we can provide them with the security they need.

Major Richard Gregory attends a local Shura with village elders.

The next phase of Op Moshtarak has already begun, with meetings with the locals set up and patrols sent out to reassure the surrounding population of the security provided by the ISAF presence.

A Shura (local meeting) was held in the patrol base and a number of local elders attended. I feel very confident that things are going well so far, both with my guys, the Afghan soldiers we are working with and the locals.

Following the Shura, the Afghan soldiers led out a joint patrol of Afghan (ANA) and 1 Royal Welsh troops into the surrounding area and the ANA platoon commander discussed the security situation with the locals.

I was really pleased with the way that patrol went. The ANA platoon commander is taking the lead. We still have to prove ourselves to the locals but we have now started that work. To say I am relieved about how things have gone so far would be an understatement. And I am bursting with pride when I see my soldiers here getting on with things that will have a really positive impact for the future of this area.

◪ A 'crow's nest' view of D Day – Operation Moshtarak

16 February 2010

Sergeant Alan Winchester, Air Traffic Control Camp Bastion, RAF

The helicopter flight line had been a hive of activity for days, with troops practising their loading drills and Engineers carrying out last-minute serviceability checks on the airframes. The pilots, British, Canadian and American, all

Sergeant Alan Winchester.

attended detailed briefs. This was vital considering the scale and complexity of the task.

When I attended the initial briefing for the operation it looked as though there were some potential 'pinch points' within the timescale envisaged. We needed to be switched on in the tower if anything unplanned happened to the Air Traffic plan because we were dealing with so many different aircraft types – Chinook, Merlin, Apache, Lynx, Canadian Griffin, Blackhawk and Sea King.

D-1: My night started off as normal at 1900 hours and without incident, setting the scene for the embarkation phase of the operation. As the sun set in Camp Bastion, my view from the tower showed row after row of helicopters on the tarmac primed and ready to go. At 0330 hours the Joint Helicopter Force lines started to gear up in darkness. D Day at last!

Below me, muted lights on the runway and blinking lights from the helicopters created a weird pattern as the dust kicked up from the ground created a hazy effect.

At the sound of over thirty rotors running I could feel the rush of excitement kick in. Finally, I was able to feel directly linked to the front line and I knew that I would be supporting, as closely as I could, the troops on the ground.

However, when the first aircraft launched calm descended and despite a few unexpected moves, all traffic departed on time and landed safely to ensure that troops reached the drop-off zones at the correct time. Wave after wave was talked out and back into Bastion as hundreds of troops and then their additional kit were ferried out into Nad-e-Ali.

I felt a distinct pride when the op launch was complete at 0600 hours and learnt that every aspect had gone to plan and had been a complete success. I left work at 0700 hours exhausted but content.

⬎ Up to our knees in mud

16 February 2010

Corporal Stephen Hall, Mortar Section Commander,

Fire Support Company, 1 Royal Welsh

As we moved off the helicopter we were expecting the terrain to be boggy, but nowhere near as bad as it was. As soon as we were off the helicopter we were up to our knees in mud. With all the weight we were carrying and the mud it was really hard going. As well as our standard kit and the mortar equipment, I also had the radio so the total weight I was carrying was huge.

Once we were on the ground I had to immediately get the light motor set up in case we were contacted or the entry into our objective needed motor fire. I was soaking wet, very cold and covered in mud, but just kept on going to make sure everything was set up straight away and ready to go.

Corporal Stephen Hall.

For my mortar section the worst bit was waiting for the initial assault section to go into the compound. We were hoping for a 'Green Knock' – when the lads go in without a shot fired – but we were sitting there in the dark, freezing and soaked to the skin, waiting for it to 'Go Red' at any time. That is the nerve-racking time for the boys.

As dawn started to break and we still weren't in, this was the time I started to get really wary. The initial section and the Afghan soldiers still hadn't got into the compound and we were all out in the open and really exposed if the insurgents opened fire.

Luckily we weren't contacted and we got in safely. Once into our objective the boys worked really hard to get everything set up in quick time. They were dog-tired and operating on their reserves by this time, but they did well.

We have now established a secure patrol base and are getting on with our task of providing mortar fire support to the troops when they need it.

So far I think Op Moshtarak seems to have gone pretty well for us and it does seem to be working, but we are just cracking on with our job now.

◥ Punching through IED belts

17 February 2010

Sergeant Major Sean Semple, Royal Engineers

Woke up after a night under the stars. No cloud cover all night. Absolutely freezing. Lying in my issue green sleeping bag – it's affectionately nicknamed the bouncing bomb – I couldn't feel my feet and hands. The sleeping bag is good, but this was cold, bloody cold.

The Engineers' job on Op Moshtarak is threefold – and all of it is critical to the success of the British end of the op.

**Sergeant Major
Sean Semple.**

Job one: punch through IED belts, ploughing or blasting our way through – after making sure no civilians can be injured, of course. To put the bad guys on the run and force them to change tactics.

Job two: build the things that we and the locals need – bridges, bases, road improvements.

Job three: push through open ground, making a path for the Logies – Logistics guys – so they can bring in much-needed supplies. For us, that means water, ammo and food for the infantry – to keep them fed and going – and starting to build new bases for Afghan troops. For local civilians, it means building equipment to get cracking with reconstruction.

With the Taliban on the back foot, or putting their weapons down and scarpering, we have a window of opportunity. We've got to take it.

Talking of the Taliban, yesterday we spent most of the day watching them watching us. Then they moved away.

Late in the afternoon, we saw something we didn't like. One of the Royal Tank Regiment sentries, Sergeant Andy Ford, saw a group of men – fighting-age males – aggressively remonstrating with a local elder. It was a good spot.

A few minutes later there was a lot of activity. The elder was hurrying the women and children out of the compound and into a vehicle. Meanwhile, two males were sitting in the field, pretending to work, but all the time looking up at our location. Interesting.

The Royal Tank Regiment's Major Mike Taylor grabbed a Quick Reaction Force – a dozen blokes and four Vikings APCs – and headed out pronto. Just as the family were heading off he got to them.

They were scared. The Taliban had kicked them out of their compound. We were being scouted for an attack, probably at night, possibly from several positions.

Major Taylor persuaded the family to stay, escorted them back to the compound and inspected it to make sure there was nothing there shouldn't be: weapons, ammo, explosives. They stayed. When the insurgents saw us coming back they legged it.

Back at our leaguer, we made sure everyone was aware of 'actions on', those are the drills that kick in when something kicks off.

A lot of good soldering is about preventing an attack, acting firmly, not sitting around and waiting. Thanks to the quick work of the Royal Tank Regiment guys, insurgents didn't take over the compound, and we got to get a decent night's sleep.

Back into my bouncing bomb. Another clear night. Stars above. Say what you like about Afghanistan, but the sky at night is truly breath-taking. I lay there thinking about my wife and kids. It was Valentine's Day recently and my thoughts were with her. When we have downtime here, I think about her and the children lots. I miss them. But when I am working, I know she wouldn't want me to be thinking about anything other than the job in hand: keeping the boys safe, getting the job done, and looking after myself too. So that's what I do.

◤ A real experience

17 February 2010

Lance Corporal Christy–Lee Ray, Royal Military Police (RMP)

attached to Fire Support Company, 1 Royal Welsh

The last week has been a real experience for me. I have been in the Army for three years now and, in addition to my RMP training, I did a whole year of special training for this tour. Just recently returned from my home leave (R&R or Rest and Recuperation), I landed back at Camp Bastion expecting to return to my job with The Rifles. However, I discovered that I was being attached to Fire Support Company, 1 Royal Welsh for Op Moshtarak.

I was genuinely excited to be part of such a massive operation, yet loading onto the helicopter in the dark and the dust on the first night I was also a bit nervous. But really you just get on with it. The entry into our objective was tough – we were cold, wet and muddy. Also, we all had to carry extra equipment as well as our normal kit. I am only 5'3" and so the weight is tough for me. The first 24 hours out here I found it quite hard, but I have got used to it now.

Currently I am one of only two females in the patrol base. The other girl has to go back to Bastion shortly so then it will be just me. However, I just muck in with it all and the lads can see that I do my job just the same as them so there is no difference between us. I do everything that they do but I am also a team medic so when we go out on patrol they will look to me if things go wrong. Working in this environment with the local people, I am also a valuable asset as a female searcher.

I won't go into the full details, but I have already started my main role which is to collect information on the local villagers and movements in the area. I then feed this information back to my boss so it can be used to build a bigger picture of conditions on the ground. It all helps in our efforts to provide a safer environment for everyone in our area of responsibility.

So far it all seems to be going really well and the locals have been friendly, helpful and seem to be on side. It is a bit strange really for life to be this quiet, but hopefully it will remain that way and I can just keep on with my job.

It is amazing how the patrol base has changed in the short time we have been here. From a bare compound when we took it on D Day, there is now a wash area, a cook area and even a makeshift gym. Most importantly, the solar showers arrived by helicopter resupply and I did enjoy having my first shower for several days.

Lance Corporal
Christy-Lee Ray.

109

⊠ IED nightmare

18 February 2010

Sergeant Major Sean Semple, Royal Engineers

It was a long day, and a tense day. Good and bad. Bad because we took two contact IEDs. Good because we sustained no injuries and the vehicles had minimal damage.

We spent the morning in our leaguer – that's where our 44-vehicles are arranged in an armoured metal box with Viking APCs and their weapons systems facing out – waiting for one of the vehicles which was involved in the strike to come back from where it was hit – about 500 metres outside our camp.

They were returning from a job, we could see them in the distance, when suddenly there was smoke, and a bang. Contact IED. We waited, concerned about the lads, but they were fine.

In the meantime we met some of the locals. Chatted to them, and we had a pretty good reception. I spoke to one of the local elders. He said he was happy we were here. This year was the first time he had grown wheat rather than poppy.

We also gave some medical assistance. Strange morning: on one side of our location we were listening to people telling us they needed schools and hospitals and wanted the Afghan Army to provide security. On the other side of the leaguer we were being IED by people wanting to kill and maim. That's Afghanistan.

We moved off in the afternoon. Driving past compounds surrounded by poppy fields. The atmospherics weren't great. Something didn't feel right. It was one of those moments when the hairs stand up on the back of your neck.

As we approached a group of compounds, the locals had vanished. Seconds later, we took another IED. The vehicle I was in had driven over the device 30 seconds before it went off.

Thank God, again no injures – in both cases the guys inside had felt a thump, the dust and sand kicked up about them, but the armour held. Although they were safe, we needed to carry out some repairs before we could get moving. And it was getting dark.

Some of the locals came out to watch. Not hostile, more curious than anything else. But we became conscious of the size of the convoy. We were a large target. In the open. In the dark.

We suspected the IED may have been a command wire IED, which would have meant Taliban in the area. We had a tense hour. Waiting for the repairs to be done, whilst keeping an eye out for anyone wanting to take us on.

In that situation you made the best of things. We put up a lot of illumination – front, sides and rear to monitor movement – as the lads cracked on. Eventually we moved and got to our new location. We breathed a sigh of relief. Like I said, it was a long day.

◪ Python first for Afghanistan

19 February 2010

Sergeant Major Sean Semple, Royal Engineers

This was one hell of a day. Almost as soon as we moved off in the morning we encountered a suspected IED belt: the strong ground signs a clear indication that the Taliban had scattered devices in front of us.

The decision was taken to fire the Python explosive hose to clear the immediate path. The Python system, attached to a Trojan tank, fires a hose filled with explosives on to a strip of ground. Seconds later it detonates, taking out any deadly improvised explosive devices that may be buried nearby.

What an explosion it was too! Two hundred metres of high explosive – a tonne and a half in all – in a hose which is fired out by a rocket on the back of the tank: awesome.

A Trojan armoured engineer tank in Helmand province. Trojan vehicles may be equipped with the Python trailer-mounted, rocket-propelled mine-clearing system.

The blokes' morale went up instantly – and shows the enemy that we mean business. The commanding officer seems particularly pleased. This kit is going to save lives. Good stuff.

In addition to clearing a safe route, the explosion also detonated at least one – probably several – devices nearby which could have killed or seriously injured the local population. This kit isn't just saving our own lives.

The locals are interested in our movement, most probably because they have never seen as many heavily armoured vehicles at once before. However, we're conscious that the Taliban are never far away. The blokes are constantly on their guard, weapons continually scanning the ground.

We drop off several non-essential vehicles at a patrol base en route, and continue to clear a route for the logistics drop-offs. Yet another find, this time a pressure plate IED in the middle of the track – uncovered this time by Trojan's special designed armoured plough – the new kit is earning its keep already.

We disabled and recovered the IED complete. We know the route ahead will be full of devices – we'll clear each one in turn. At the same time, a section of Engineers repaired some of the local infrastructure. Dealing with bombs and improving the roads – Afghans can see for themselves that we are here to make the place safer and better.

Night-time location is a field, and a bloody muddy one. But it's clear of IEDs so it's safe. We arrive in the dark and go straight into night routine. The blokes are tired, but it has been a good day. The enemy, they know where we are, but we have the protection to deal with whatever they throw at us.

Not too cold tonight, a big bonus. You can deal with anything as long as you know that you have a warm sleeping system to climb into at the end of the day. Tea consists of boil in the bag rations: vegetable madras with some extra curry powder thrown in.

As an instructor in the Army Physical Training Corps, this couldn't be more different from my normal day-to-day job, I suppose it goes to show how diverse the Army is these days, and soldiers are becoming more adaptable in whatever role they have to fulfil.

Four days in and it's all going well, long may this continue, however long we are out for.

↘ It's going to make one hell of a bang when it goes off!

19 February 2010

Sergeant Jason Thrasher, 32 Regiment Royal Artillery,

Unmanned Aerial Vehicle (UAV) Image Analyst

It is day four and I am watching a bank of large screens in front of me. The black and white images are crystal clear, showing me a bird's eye view of the mighty Python moving into position on one screen, and a foot patrol of Afghan troops and Royal Welsh soldiers on patrol in a different location on another screen.

Sergeant Jason Thrasher.

The Python is about to clear an area of suspected IEDs along the new route being created into Nad-e-Ali, heading towards the key town of Showal. This is the first time that it is being used in Afghanistan and a small audience has gathered behind me to see what happens.

In another cabin next to the Operations Room the 'pilot' of the un-manned Hermes 450 is flying the aircraft directly over the Manoeuvre Support Group, 28 Regiment Royal Engineers. He looks like he is playing on a grown-up version of a play station as he deftly guides the UAV over the tactical position on the ground.

We are in constant communication with each other because as I watch the images I can talk him through adjusting the flight path so that I can scan the whole area. My job is to make absolutely sure that there are no local Afghans, military personnel or rural compounds in the blast area. It is going to make one hell of a bang when it goes off!

Image Analysis can be a nervous business! If you make a wrong call, lives could be lost. So you have to 'Confirm in your head ... confirm in your head ... confirm in your head' before you make any decision.

I confirm that the area is clear for firing.

The message is relayed to the troops on the ground, and as I watch from Camp Bastion, the Python lets rip! I can't hear the sound but the black and white image in front of me explodes in an impressive cloud of dust.

Job done. Back to providing over-watch of the foot patrol as it carefully makes its way through another area of Nad-e-Ali. Our task to hold a secure area in central Helmand continues, with everyone working hard to keep the Taliban out and bring the civilian stabilisation teams in.

◩ Fighting to build bridges

20 February 2010

Sergeant Major Sean Semple, Royal Engineers

A slightly frustrating day: full of problems but productive in the end. We were up before first light. Every sinew of you wants to stay inside the sleeping bag, but we needed to crack on clearing the proposed logistic supply route – one of our key tasks.

We made a bit of progress – then another IED, dug into the route in front of us. We dealt with it without incident. Back home the public only hear about the few IEDs that go off, injuring or killing guys. What they don't see are the dozens that we find and make safe. It's a coward's way to fight a war: indiscriminate. No wonder the locals around here hate the insurgents. They just want peace.

Next problem: there's a large ditch on the route. We could just fill it in and move on, but that would damage an Afghan farmer's livelihood. So we decide to bridge it instead, which means calling in a Chinook carrying an under-slung bridge.

Again, what the public don't see is the incredible lengths we go to to build bridges – forgive the pun – with the Afghan people. We could go quicker and give the insurgents less time to plant IEDs, but that would mean upsetting local people, and the Engineers are here to improve the route, not trash it.

We wait for the Chinook and observe our arcs – i.e. making sure we're covered in case of ambush. We also chat with the locals.

We give the children sweets and compensate a farmer for driving over his wheat crop – good on him for not planting poppies. I have kids myself, and when I see these Afghan children living such a primitive existence, it makes me want something better for them. This is a world away from how we live our lives.

The commanding officer showed the locals a Girls Aloud video on his iPod. Their eyes almost popped out, they loved it – bet they've never seen that before in Helmand. The boss told us it was on his iPod because his kids put it there. I have my doubts though.

It prompted a long debate between the lads as to who was the best looking in the group: Kimberly came out as the overall winner. The commanding officer has invited them to the after-tour party, but we've yet to get a reply. We agreed that he must be a closet Girls Aloud fan.

The Chinook came in with two Apache attack helicopters for protection. What a great sight! Engineers love this sort of stuff. They like it on exercise but to do it for real on Operations is another experience altogether – even under the watchful eye of Taliban 'scouts'.

Gently, the Chinook lowered the bridge into position and we set about constructing the finishing touches – all that lifting and carrying we did on pre-tour physical training paid off. The boys were all over it and glad of the exercise too.

It was last light when we finished. We set up the vehicles in all round defence. Meatballs and pasta for evening meal, and then into my sleeping bag.

I think of all the things I'm looking forward to after the tour.

We didn't get as far as we wanted, but we did put in a bridge which will be used by the Logistics girls and guys to resupply forward operating bases, and for the locals to get produce to market: a little victory for hearts and minds, so crucial for this campaign.

◪ Life is busy

21 February 2010
Captain Anna Crossley, Queen Alexandra's Royal Army Nursing Corps,
Inkerman Company, Grenadier Guards

Sharzad, central Helmand, is a long way from the green hills of the Brecon Beacons, but here I am, the first female Nursing Officer the Grenadiers have ever had! It's taken them a bit of time to get used to the idea, but the lads will pop in to see me to discuss any problems they have or just have a chat. I hope this shows that they have accepted me as part of the team.

I'd already spent three months working in Bastion, so I've come across pretty much every type of injury you can imagine, which is extremely useful preparation for this job out at the patrol base, where every injury, no matter how serious, will be initially dealt with by me and my team.

The soldiers here have been busy for the last few weeks. Before Op Moshtarak kicked off last weekend they were carrying out what we call 'shaping' operations – basically setting up and reinforcing checkpoints in the area to deny the insurgents freedom of movement. And this week they have been full tilt on Op Moshtarak, going beyond the original front line into Taliban-held territory.

Back at base, the majority of the work I do is primary care: treating minor ailments and making sure the troops are combat effective, that is to say, they are not prevented from doing their job by illnesses and ailments. But we are always at a high state of readiness to deal with more serious injuries.

We maintain constant contact with the Operations Room, which is the nerve centre of our patrol base, so that we are prepared to receive the patients when they arrive, but if I hear a loud bang I will always pop next door to see if we are going to be needed.

I have a team of combat medics who are on the ground and work as part of the patrolling teams. They are first on the

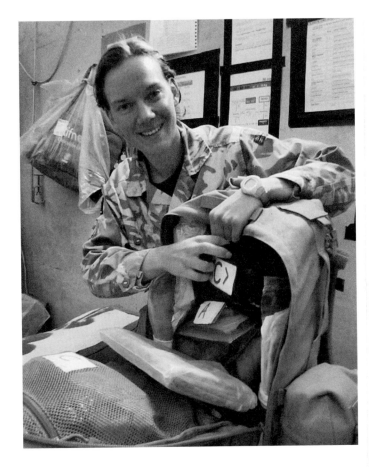

Captain Anna Crossley.

scene and play a vital role in delivering first aid in the crucial first few minutes when something happens.

Sharzad was the original American HQ for the team that led the irrigation scheme in the 1950s. It was this scheme that created the fertile Green Zone that runs down the Helmand River valley today. So the building we operate from is a solid 1950s brick and stone build, with all the original plans, drawings and records still here.

The facility we run is unique within the UK context. It is effectively a mini Accident and Emergency Department and we carry an extensive range of specialist kit to be able to treat people in this location. We also stabilise any more serious casualties for forward transit to Camp Bastion and the full working hospital that is located there.

Life is busy, but the job satisfaction when we save a life out here is immeasurable.

◩ Thought for the day

21 February 2010

Padre Mark Christian, Senior Chaplain

Last night here in Lashkar Gah, in the tent that is our church, we had a simple Holy Communion service, drawing crosses of ash on our foreheads and saying the traditional words from the Ash Wednesday service which marks the beginning of Lent: 'Remember that you are dust, and to dust you shall return. Turn away from sin and be faithful to Christ.'

I am not sure if you could say there's ever a good time to come out on military operations, but the season of Lent reflects the atmosphere here better than any other church season. The men and women serving here live a very simple and basic existence.

All the distractions and many of the comforts of home are missing. Everybody works relentlessly, but in the times you do have to yourself, living this life helps you focus on what is important – family and loved ones at home, of course, but also the people around you, who serve with you, and upon whom you depend – sometimes to keep you alive.

At the heart of the Lent theme is sacrifice. A quality that's paramount to any soldier, but especially at a time like this, during a major operation. The concept of sacrifice is so important to the Army that it appears as 'selfless commitment' in our six core values.

Every day, soldiers in Helmand put themselves in harm's way for the sake of the security of our nation and to bring peace to Afghanistan:

Camp Bastion
Memorial to
all those who
have fallen in
Helmand province.

The young Rifleman who knows that he will be attacked almost every time he leaves his patrol base.

Every soldier, who in the face of the enemy understands that he is expected to show 'courageous restraint' – not to open fire if there is any chance of civilians being killed, even if this puts him in greater danger.

The courage, the fear, the sacrifice, the loss of friends and the hard-won successes, amongst other things, make a tour of duty in Afghanistan an emotionally intensive 6 months. It changes everyone who serves here – not necessarily in the negative ways that you'll hear on the news or read in the papers, but it deepens our understanding of life because everyday in one way or another we reflect on, and are challenged by, issues of morality, mortality, faith and human relationships.

On my recent leave I visited some patients at Selly Oak hospital. I was talking to one recently injured soldier for over an hour. He was talking about his friends – the ones who had died and the ones he had fought with. About how scared he was, but how he knew he had to go on.

At the end of the conversation I noticed that he was holding one of the brigade dog tags that his chaplain had given him. He read from the verse of scripture that is on the back of the tag from Joshua chapter 1 verse 9 – 'I will be strong and courageous. I will not be terrified or discouraged; for the Lord my God is with me wherever I go'. He looked at me and said, 'Do you think I have been strong and courageous, padre?'

I think you can guess how I answered him.

◪ Taliban flag hauled down

22 February 2010

Major Richard Gregory, Fire Support Company, 1 Royal Welsh

The Company and our Afghan Army partners have now firmly established a patrol base, east of Garbay Noray in Nad-e-Ali, Helmand province.

For the first couple of days we focused on base security and defensive positions. This involved clearing all the compound areas and surrounding routes for IEDs, filling and placing sandbags for firing points and setting up a home from home in the base. A cooking area, washing area, toilet and even an improvised gym were all quickly created to make life bearable.

By the second day we had started to build positive relationships with the elders and families in the area, holding local Shuras to discuss their needs and concerns. Meanwhile, our Afghan partners proudly raised the Afghanistan flag to fly above the Camp.

However, out on the ground the front line was still clearly marked. For four days a plain white Taliban flag has flown just 300 metres away from the patrol base, an area where only a few of the locals are willing to go. In much of the area the threat of IEDs remains high.

As the Counter-IED Team came in and cleared a route through the area, the next phase of Operation Moshtarak, the 'hold', is beginning to take effect. The daily Shuras held by myself are bringing the locals on side. And the regular joint patrols, led by the Afghan Army, are showing that security is being brought back to the area.

Today, the fifth day of Op Moshtarak, Afghan soldiers moved in unopposed and took down the Taliban flag, removing the remaining symbol of insurgent control in the area. Another symbol of success on this operation, and out on the front line another small victory for ISAF and the Afghan National Army.

◪ Everything was going smoothly

23 February 2010

Sergeant Colin Pentith, Royal Logistic Corps, Fire Support Company,

1 Royal Welsh

We had been on the ground for three days and, so far, everything was going very smoothly. The boys were into a

Sergeant Colin Pentith greets a local.

good routine and the locals had started to actively engage with us throughout the area. The challenge for me now was to lead a Shura at a checkpoint established by the Afghan Army and Fire Support Company, 1 Royal Welsh, east of Garbay Noray.

This was to be my first Shura. A far cry from my usual job as a Royal Logistic Corps Chef! The transition from hotplate to hot stabilisation really began last year when I got selected to work with 1 Royal Welsh as part of its non-combat role in what we call 'influence'. Effectively, it is working with other non-military organisations and the locals to make progress through communication, information and initiating local projects.

The elders I met treated me with respect and what struck me from the meeting we held was that the concerns of the locals are just what you would expect anywhere. They are concerned about security first and then basic welfare – schools, hospitals, power and so on. It is up to us to reassure them that we and the Afghan National Security Services will deliver that. This was also the start of our process of getting to know who is who in the local area so that we can identify the key leaders that will make things happen.

Afterwards, as part of the stabilisation process, we distributed blankets and radios together with footballs and pens for the children. They genuinely seemed happy and there were lots of smiling faces so I think it went well. It made me feel good that, having come into their area as a 'foreign' soldier, I could make a small but positive difference straight away.

A night on the edge of a graveyard

23 February 2010

Sergeant Major Sean Semple, Royal Engineers

We spent last night on the outskirts of the largest graveyard in Helmand province; nice.

The day started well. We got all the vehicles across the bridge we'd flown in the day before, so the lads' hard work was worth it.

We cautiously continued our move – down a route no ISAF vehicle has seen for a year. We dismounted and patrolled along a track, assessing potential vulnerable points – the places the insurgents are most likely to plant IEDs – and also where our vehicles could potentially cause damage to the heavy mud compound walls and dusty roads.

Patrolling down the track we heard heavy gun fire to our east and west, so we were definitely on our guard.

Moving on, we reinforce every point the track crosses a drainage ditch to cope with the increased weight of the resupply trucks in the logistics convoys following us. This took most of the day.

Each time repair was required it drew locals from all over the area. They watched the Engineers' every movement and seemed to converse amongst themselves about how we were improving the local infrastructure.

One of the local elders asked for a shot of the sledgehammer and assisted with the repairs. Nice touch – another little victory – and some happy local faces.

There's no doubt the locals are pleased to see us, but they need convincing that we will stay. We need to prove to them that they can live and function without the Taliban – then they'll have no place here anymore.

The Viking support group from the Royal Tank Regiment is providing our flank protection. What an awesome job these guys are doing. With their armoured and highly mobile vehicles, they are not afraid to go anywhere, so there's no hiding place for the enemy.

We arrived at our admin area for the night. For once we're in place before it gets dark. We've been out six days now.

The more the weather heats up during the day – and it's been getting quite hot the last few days – the more we are sweating, so no doubt we're all smelling lovely!

Karl, our driver, cooked an awesome scoff. It was a famous Army 'all in' – loads of ration packs in a pan, cooked together with some Tabasco sauce and curry powder thrown in. I wouldn't choose it from a restaurant menu, but it was great all the same. We learn later about the sad loss of two more British colleagues. It makes you think that it could so easily have been one of us. Our thoughts are with their loved ones. Rest in peace, lads.

◨ Reflections on Operation Ghartse Ghadmahe, Sangin, Northern Helmand

24 February 2010

Major Tim Harris, Officer Commanding A Company, 3 RIFLES

As I look out across the Sangin Green Zone from forward operating base Nolay, I see green shoots. Perhaps it is too soon to describe them as the 'green shoots of recovery', but the seasons are changing and the wheat and poppy crops are beginning to appear; they represent a sign of hope. Most of the fields near me are wheat: the Afghan Government's wheat seed distribution last October was widely seized upon, although hopes of any altruism behind the local farmers' choice of crop are wide of the mark.

Major Tim Harris.

They grow wheat because it is profitable, nothing more. The fields are busy – farming here is labour intensive and involves these hardy people stooping for hour after hour, nursing their precious crops by hand. This makes it doubly difficult for a soldier to identify who is a farmer and who might be laying an improvised explosive device. If we are not sure, we will observe them and make a note of the area so that we might treat it with caution when we next patrol there. But my men now have a good idea of what constitutes 'farming' and what is more nefarious. The Afghan soldiers we work with are even more culturally tuned in; together we form a strong team, which is the essence of embedded partnering.

There have been dark days, days when our luck has deserted us, but I am confident that there have been more days when the enemy must have felt that fate was conspiring against him. We have given him a bloody nose on more than one occasion, and more importantly he is no longer able to patrol the agricultural Green Zone to our west with impunity, weapons on show to scare the locals. They are still around and among us, and are still hell bent on intimidating the people and stopping us from achieving our goals, but the Rifleman is a resolute beast, and does not scare easily.

It is very easy after we take a casualty to find yourself asking, 'Are we doing the right thing?' The answer, most definitely, is 'Yes'. Progress can be hard to measure in counter-insurgency: the metrics are often difficult to define. In 'conventional' war fighting, we can measure success by yards gained, relative body counts and key enemy equipments destroyed. It is easy to demonstrate progress.

However, in a counter-insurgency battle where the people are the prize, how do you measure victories, when a victory may simply be a local who decides in his own mind to stop hosting out of area fighters? It is difficult to show graphically how Sangin 'feels' better over time. It is sometimes worth going back into old reports and comparing them with today's circumstances; in doing so I have realised that areas in the summer that would only have been visited at Company strength are now patrolled by platoons, or even sections. As a barometer of success this is encouraging. But the question we now have to answer is: can the progress that has been made during the winter be maintained over the summer?

Talk of a 'fighting season' misses the point. The insurgency is locally based with support from outside (whether foreign countries or other areas of Afghanistan). Contrary to popular myth, most of the insurgents we fight do not pack up and go home for the winter period. They are locals, who fight for a wide variety of reasons: vengeance for the death of a family member, money, status, coercion, or in some instances for fun.

The summer brings with it the complexity of the maize crop, which will replace the wheat and poppy that I now see growing. The maize provides, well, a maze for the insurgents to move about in. Up to ten feet high, it is a serious issue. If the gains that have been made over the winter are to be held throughout the summer by our successors, the Royal Marines, we must provide a solution now, perhaps dwarf varieties of maize that will give the locals a profitable crop that can feed their families and make some money, but do not obscure fields of view.

The seasons change, time marches on and the wheat serves as a daily reminder that the maize is coming too. If we get this right, we can really begin to 'take the fun out of fighting' for the insurgents, and make further steady demonstrable progress, however glacially slow that progress may sometimes appear.

Back from the front

24 February 2010

Sergeant Major Sean Semple, Royal Engineers

There is the slightest chance that we might complete all our tasks today and head back into Camp Bastion tonight, morale is on the up.

Our task today is to clear a route in order for the Royal Engineers to build a bridge over a large river, so the Trojan tank leads the way to the bridge build site. The bridge is not only going to provide an essential crossing point for the resupply of the forward patrol bases, but it will also enhance the quality of life for the local nationals.

The current method of crossing the river consists of pieces of wood bound together to act as a raft and a length of rope with which to pull yourself across. Primitive but effective all the same.

It is certainly a lot hotter today; there is a far greater need to consume water when out on the ground in the heat. For a soldier to go down with a heat-related injury not only presents his colleagues with the additional burden of being a man down, but potentially the need for one if not more to provide critical medical assistance also.

The climate in this place is mad; it can be below freezing at night-time and absolutely roasting hot during the day.

The face and neck is building up a nice bit of colour, the nose taking the brunt of the sun, the resemblance to Rudolph just now is strikingly similar. I can almost hear the lecture from my wife about putting sun cream on. The rest of the body remains proudly Scottish white though.

After the bridge is assembled successfully, the decision is taken to head back to Camp Bastion to allow the Vikings group to prepare for their next task. A long and dusty drive through the desert follows, we drive past a US Counter-IED Team disposing of a device in the middle of nowhere – these bloody IEDs are everywhere.

As we arrive in Camp Bastion, we are met by Sergeant Major Taff Williams, who greets us warmly and is pleased to see us back in one piece. His relief is very quickly replaced by sarcastic mickey-taking about appearing in the paper, squaddies do not do publicity very well.

First off the vehicles are the weapons, ammunition, and personal equipment. Absolutely everything is covered in sand; all the kit is emptied and separated, some equipment is handed back in straight away after a quick clean.

A shower later on comes as welcome relief, as does coffee and further squaddie banter.

Although the Manoeuvre Support Group (MSG) is back in camp, there are still many more soldiers still out on the ground playing crucial roles in continuing to provide safety and improved infrastructure to the people of Afghanistan. These guys do not have the luxury of having a shower, or relaxing in relative comfort. Weeks to go for the troops on this tour are getting few, and most will allow themselves to think about what they intend to spend their well-earned post op tour leave doing. There are still many hurdles to jump until the tour is over, but you can rest assured that we are all doing our level best over here.

◩ Hot showers and fresh food

25 February 2010

Major Mike Taylor, D Squadron, 1 Royal Tank Regiment,

Manoeuvre Support Group

We are back in from the first phase of Op Moshtarak and it is great to be back in camp with hot showers and fresh food.

The last few weeks have been a real experience working as part of the Manoeuvre Support Group; a combination of Viking Armoured Personnel Carriers and the heavy engineering vehicles of 28 Engineer Regiment, whose job was to clear a major route into the strategic town of Showal, a settlement with a reputation for being a drug trading haven, as well as the 'seat' of government for the Taliban.

During the pre-operational training we really bonded together well. Our role was to provide the firepower and protect the slow-moving column of vehicles. So we had to practise our

drills together to allow the Engineers to do their job: using new equipment to plough through or explode IED belts, build bridges, fix roads, etc.

I'm a tankie by training. I've got D Squadron of the Royal Tank Regiment out here. We miss our Challenger tanks, but the guys love the Viking Armoured Personnel Carriers and they actually enjoy being out on the ground.

On D Day, several hours after the helicopter assault went in, we trundled out from Camp Bastion with my Vanguard Force in front. They are a very strong, cohesive troop commanded by Lieutenant Anthony Kaulbeck, who had to guide us safely around or through the areas laid with IEDs. He recce'd along less obvious routes to avoid classic ambush points, searching for signs of unusual human activity on the ground. I have to say that Ant has a particular talent for this. Of the 35 IEDs that the Viking Group has discovered, he has been responsible for at least half of them. Life-saving stuff really.

Our most rewarding moment of the long route clearance came on day two when we were observing arcs around the leaguer (that's the place where our 44-vehicle convoy was located, Viking APCs around the outside to provide a 'metal fort', with Engineering vehicles in the middle), when one of the guys on sentry, Sergeant Andy Ford, picked up abnormal behaviour in a field 200 metres away.

It was three young men and an elder. What was odd was that the men were acting aggressively towards the elder, pointing and remonstrating, which is a disrespectful way to carry on in a culture that respects age. The elder went back to his compound and soon a people carrier appeared. There was a lot of activity; the women and children were bundled into the vehicle. Meanwhile, the men in the field were pretending to work, bending down and sowing seeds, but all the time looking up at the leaguer location.

We suspected that the men were insurgents, and their likely plan was to take over the nearby family compound to use as

Viking Armoured Personnel Carrier.

a firing position that night. I immediately broke out a Viking Quick Reaction Force (QRF) and headed to the compound. We managed to get there and stop the family leaving. And although they said that there were no insurgents around, their fear was palpable. They wanted to get out.

We talked calmly to them and searched the compound. In the meantime, the three young men had run away. The local people relaxed slightly. We reassured them that ISAF and Afghan forces were moving into the area to stay. In the end we got a decent night's sleep without the small arms attack which had been brewing. Prevention was better than a firefight in this situation.

The locals do seem to want us here, but understandably are worried about the transition period when the Taliban still have influence. I have never spoken to a local who, in private, has a good word to say about the Taliban and the influence they hold in society. Maybe they are saying it because they are talking to ISAF, but I sense that people are starting to realise we are not necessarily the bad guys in all this.

Over the next few days we continued to provide protection as the Royal Engineers used Trojan to plough a new main route, and Python was deployed and detonated to clear a particularly difficult point with multiple IEDs on the ground. A couple of bridges were laid to improve the route access until, finally, we drove into the town of Showal and linked up with A Company, 1 Royal Welsh. They had spent the week securing the town following their helicopter insertion and were very glad to see us because the route we had just cleared was soon to be used by the Logistics guys bringing in fresh food, water, equipment and vital materials to build a proper patrol base.

⬎ Back at Bastion

26 February 2010

Trooper Pete Sheppard, Brigade Reconnaissance Force (BRF)

We arrived back in Camp Bastion at supper time last night, having finished the first phase of Op Moshtarak. I'm part of the Squadron HQ element of the BRF, so we drove back to camp and arrived yesterday evening. The rest of the troops were still clearing out on the ground and didn't get back until late evening.

The last 10 days have been hard work. The fields out on the ground are being irrigated at the moment so they are very boggy. Some of the guys were sinking up to their knees.

Trooper Pete Sheppard.

Limbu, our friendly Gurkha from the Queen's Own Gurkha Logistics Regiment, we call them 'Loggies', stepped into a large muddy ditch waiting for the helicopter pick-up. In the dark his section didn't notice him flailing around trying to get out. He tried to take his heavy Bergen off to pull himself out but only managed to plant his face into the mud! It took two guys to go back and pull him out. I wish I had got a picture of him caked from head to foot! Everyone was knackered! But glad to be back in camp to have a shower and eat normal food. Some went to the cookhouse, but for many Camp Bastion's own form of Pizza Hut was the favourite choice.

The boxes sent from friends and family at home were also a real treat to come back to. They are great, and the lads raid them for toiletries, biscuits, sweets and chewing gum. We just about had time to visit the NAAFI to get all the little things like chocolate, pop and noodles – anything to break the routine of ration packs. Though, with things heating up out here, the chocolate isn't going to last long anymore.

After a sound night's sleep, it was back down to our compound to replen (sort out!) the vehicles in preparation for going straight out again. The lads think it is going to be a hangout over the next few days. Lots of tabbing (what we call marching) and long days in general out on the ground. But while things are going well we want to keep at it. We are leaving soon, so it is the last-minute vehicle and kit checks, then off we go!

◪ Identifying insurgents on the Afghan front line

27 February 2010

Trooper Pete Sheppard, BRF

It was an early start this morning. Everyone only had about four hours' kip – minus an hour on stag duty.

We leaguered up (putting the vehicles in a defensive formation) on the outside of a small patrol base close to the area we would be going into to exploit over the next few days. The base is surrounded by a wall of Hesco [flat pack metal mesh]. This provides protection to the people inside; but it seems we are on the outside providing greater security for the base.

The troops left early this morning on clearance patrols. However, no insurgents were seen nor even any evidence of them. A small number of the compounds had been set up with IEDs, but the lads spotted these and information got passed up informing the headquarters of the situation on the ground.

We are aware that the insurgents are watching us, which is frustrating, as we can't visually identify them unless they are doing something incriminating. However, attached to us are the Afghan Task Force, and they are able to spot someone who is suspicious and pick up on the small things that look out of place. It really makes a difference having them with us and we rely on their local and cultural knowledge.

When the guys got back, we started our routine, which included grabbing the opportunity to catch up on sleep before the next day.

One of the guys on my wagon, Donny, is due home in 28 days today. He is sure to remind us each day of this countdown to see if people bite. He is a funny guy and has a small boy back home who is very mischievous going by the stories he tells me of him. Just chatting like this I think everyone is keen now to return home and see our family and friends.

But the good thing about the armed forces is the guys you work with; the banter and the jokes. Squaddies have their own sense of humour which most of the time can only be appreciated by other squaddies. And when we are out on tense operations like this, it is vital that our sense of humour is maintained.

We will be out here for a few days and this area is not fully cleared of insurgents, so it will be interesting what tomorrow brings. In the meantime, another lad called Joe that I work with likes to give us a riddle to try to solve. It gives us something to think about whilst on stag. So here is today's ...

What goes up a drainpipe down, but not down a drainpipe up?

⧉ It will be a success if it is a total anti-climax

27 February 2010

Sergeant Major Greg Reece, Royal Artillery, Military Stabilisation and Support

'It will be a success if it is a total anti-climax.'

That was what we were told. In reality we planned for a big fight, platoon size, out of area fighters willing to stand their ground. All roads IED'd. Possibly IED'd helicopter landing sites.

First light on a cold morning on the outskirts of Naquilabad Kalay and the insertion had gone better than expected. No IEDs, no firing, a slightly longer walk than expected, thanks to the RAF, and we were looking down the main street of the town ... from a safe distance.

Suppose we better go and meet the locals; a small group of curious Afghans were stood at the edge of town wondering what all the fuss was about. After talking with them for a very short time we realised these weren't the 'out of area' fighters we were expecting and they invited us to walk with them down the high street. They really wanted to show off their town. The commander agreed and Neil (our intelligence officer) and I were leading the patrol, carried on a wave of people that slowly grew until we reached the town centre.

We were invited to hold an impromptu Shura for 300 locals. I remember looking at my watch. It was 1000 hrs on D Day. I'm sure we're not supposed to be here doing this until D+10, maybe later; what are we going to do with the next 9 days?

Total anti-climax. If you were looking for a fight it most definitely was an anti-climax. If, like me, you were supposed to stabilise and support the local community, it was the exact opposite.

Sergeant Major Greg Reece. [Picture: Major Paul Smyth]

What we found in Naquilabad Kalay was a thriving (if not scared) community. Well-kept trees lined the main street with hand pump wells every 20 metres. Good irrigation, healthy people, healthy animals. In fact, quite an affluent society, happy to see ISAF, just needing a bit of security – thank you very much. So, job done; everyone happy, hand your bedding in, we can all go home! Don't know what all the fuss is about!

The truth is, however, what do I do now? My job is not to rebuild lives, homes and jobs. That's done. A little bit of security, thank you very much. Maybe they could do with a leisure centre!!!

◪ Open for business in Showal

28 February 2010

Squadron Leader Dee Taylor, RAF, Media Ops

By the end of February over half the bazaar in Showal is open for business, with more shops opening on a daily basis. This is a complete change of fortune. Prior to Op Moshtarak the bazaar had been closed entirely, primarily due to the threat of IEDs.

Local Afghan people are being sent the message through Shuras and the local radio station that stalls are stocked and that coalition forces are constantly patrolling the area. And word is getting out.

However, at a recent Shura local people are still worried about the threat of IEDs along the village roads leading into Showal. The Afghan National Civil Order Police Commander at Showal, Colonel Abdul Mohammed, said, 'We are here to provide reassurance and security'.

Security patrols are 'de rigeur' in Showal, and for A Company, 1 Royal Welsh, and there is a keenness to ensure routes are clear and to encourage people to use the market. The Afghan National Army play no small part in these patrols, with their numbers weighted at 60% of the patrol.

There is an abundance of shops and stalls open, ranging from fresh produce to footballs. And certainly the meat-seller was doing brisk business; not least amongst his customers were ANA soldiers. 'The food here is good, and so very fresh,' said Narjeev, the second in command of the Afghan National Army Company in Showal. To prove a point, members of the British forces were invited to dine, on a regular basis, with their Afghan hosts at supper time.

The opening of the bazaar has been welcomed by locals. A local elder said he had to travel as far as Lashkar Gah for food, which could take up to four hours in a round trip. Now

his family have access again to the bazaar and he is very keen that people should be able to shop locally.

Elders in the village are spreading the word that the locals should feel confident to shop at the bazaar, but also feeding back to ISAF that they must continue to provide security. It is a message that is not lost on A Company commander, Major Sean Hackney, whose aim 'is to restore business as usual, pre-Taliban intimidation'. So on a security footing and commercial footing, progress is definitely being made, with growth in the number of stallholders touting for business being more palpable on a daily basis.

Afghans at a local market in Showal. [Picture: Squadron Leader Dee Taylor]

↘ Contact IED ... We have a casualty

28 February 2010

Trooper Pete Sheppard, BRF

The BRF is outside a small patrol base and the vehicles are in a close-knit formation. The surrounding area is rural, a lot of farming fields around us with a series of compounds in the near distance.

Our task on this operation is to find, fix and exploit any insurgents in the area. Over the last couple of days we have been conducting clearance patrols, moving through compounds methodically. There is a small canal about 3 metres wide just in front of us running north to south.

Other than that, the area around is still quite dry. There hasn't been any large amount of rain for a while, only short, light bursts. Everyone was up for 0345 hours this morning to go out on more clearance patrols. Then at about 0615, there was a big explosion. Everyone looked at each other instantly. Then over the radio net came 'CONTACT IED!' Another look of shock came across our faces.

Seconds later – 'We have a casualty!' Everyone went quiet, then, 'It's Foxy!' The adrenaline and training kicked in. We started to prep the '9 liner', a situation report needed to send up the chain of command to make them aware of what had happened and of the injuries sustained.

Moments later, the medivac helicopter was wheels up from Camp Bastion. Over the radio net – 'he's in a bad way!' Again, we looked at each other.

The guys still in our position were just shaking their heads. No words were said. From my position in squadron headquarters it was so frustrating not being right there and able to react with the guys; I felt helpless being positioned a bit further back.

However, I know my job as a radio operator is very important, passing up all the vital information, especially with an incident like this. Still, I wished I could be there to help more. Over the insurgents' radios we heard them congratulating each other for the attack. I let out a few expletives. 'I hope the lads bloody smash these guys!' I said.

Everyone looked very annoyed at their boasting and I'm sure they were thinking similar things. After the helicopter landed and Foxy was airlifted away the troops came under small arms fire.

This is not typical of insurgent activity as we had an Apache helicopter overhead and the insurgents normally, very rightly so, are scared of it. A few moments later they went back into hiding, unwilling to risk getting spotted by the Apache. They called over their radios for more back-up. Roughly 15 minutes later the boss heard confirmation over the radio – 'Your casualty is KIA'.

I looked at Donny (who had just replaced me on the radio stag) in disbelief, willing him to say that I had misheard it. He just looked down and shook his head.

The troops continued to be engaged with small arms and a rocket-propelled grenade (RPG) until approximately 0900, and then it went quiet. We then proceeded to advance and the lads began searching local compounds. However, nothing and no one had been found by lunchtime.

The insurgents were tantalisingly close. Over their radios they declared that they could see us, they claimed they were starting to mass troops, that they were going to stop us from leaving and that they were ready to start firing at us. All talk, because once again it was a quiet, albeit sombre afternoon. The troops on the ground weren't officially told of Foxy's death until they had all returned in from the patrol. This was to prevent them from not thinking straight.

The boss was told first and he then told the corporal major. Moments later, the squadron corporal major (SCM) called

Sergeant Paul Fox.

everyone over and told them the news. Everyone was shocked and peed off. It is hard losing a character like him from the team. We stayed in our small leaguer for the remainder of the day with no more patrols going out.

At about 1900 we held a service in the field, not far from where he had fallen, in memory of Sergeant Paul 'Foxy' Fox. It started with the SCM saying, 'Right, everyone gather round. The Fijians are going to do a service and a few prayers for Foxy.' Jon Jon, one of the Fijians, said a few words about him. Then Rocko read a verse from the Bible, Book of Psalms, Chapter 91.

Jon Jon then went into what this verse meant. After this, the group of Fijian soldiers started to sing an amazing hymn called 'I need Thee, O I need Thee'. They sang this in English to start off with and then for the last verse they sang it in Fijian. Fijian choir singing is phenomenal. It really touched us all, the harmony of their song. It was blissfully quiet everywhere, all that could be heard were these soldiers singing in remembrance.

A mortar illumination round was then fired from our 81mm mortar to mark the start of a minute's silence. Everyone jumped at the loud bang it made. Emotions were deep at this moment, thinking about Foxy and even the little things, like the last thing he said to me – asking me if I had any spare sugar for his brew, and then thanking me afterwards. Another mortar round bellowed out breaking the silence.

Then the officer commanding came to the centre and read a poem:

> Do not stand at my grave and weep,
> I am not there, I do not sleep;
> I am a thousand winds that blow,
> I am the diamond glints on snow.
> I am the sunlight on ripening grain,
> I am the gentle autumn rain.
> When you awaken in the morning hush,
> I am the swift uplifting rush
> Of quiet birds in circled flight
> I am the soft stars that shine at night.
> Do not stand at my grave and cry
> I am not there, I did not die.

It was a very moving poem. The SCM said, 'Right everyone, now's the time to go away and talk about the fond memories we all have of Foxy. When we go to Cyprus we'll have a drink for him and when we get back to Windsor, after the medals parade, we'll have a toast.'

⬃ We probably saved someone's life ...

1 March 2010

Trooper Pete Sheppard, BRF

It was relatively quiet for the remainder of the day yesterday, but the evening was a time to reflect and remember. Then, at 2030 hrs, we managed to get eyes on four people digging and loitering around the area of the IED strike that caused our casualty.

We were able to positively identify them as insurgents by using both our air assets and observation equipment, and we observed them replanting another IED. We were also able to track them moving away to their night-time location. Again, another early start this morning, we were up at 0215!

The troops went out on a patrol to go and introduce themselves to the insurgents at their compound ... The insurgents mounted a heavy resistance, using automatic weapons and grenades, but were quickly subdued by our guys. We were able to obtain a lot of evidence, including weapons and radios. A great result today! Everyone is chuffed with the positive strike.

We did have a minor casualty when gaining entry but he is going to be fine. Everyone is tired. We are just going to rest for the remainder of the day, whilst waiting to send the evidence and the detainees back up the chain of command for questioning and investigation.

Our American Explosive Ordnance Disposal team, which has been frequently attached to us, went on a further patrol and dealt with the IED that was replanted by the insurgents last night. Again another great find – we probably saved someone's life by finding it and removing the device – and are particularly pleased to have captured the insurgents who laid it.

Another day down. One less to go. Oh, and just in case you didn't crack it – Answer to [Saturday's] riddle: an umbrella.

◪ No mean feat

1 March 2010

Lance Corporal Jeevan Rai, Queen's Own Gurkha Logistics Regiment

It was 0400 and there were people everywhere preparing vehicles and checking routes. Whilst noisy and busy, each vehicle knew exactly where it fitted into the convoy to resupply A Company, 1 Royal Welsh, at Showal. We were not only taking resupplies, but bringing in building equipment to build a new patrol base at Showal.

This was no mean feat as there were 59 vehicles and 188 people involved in the move. We were one of the vehicles

Lance Corporal Jeevan Rai checks the ground for any IED threats. [Picture: Squadron Leader Dee Taylor]

at the front of the convoy and were there to provide force protection. I was in charge of Whiskey 3, the codename for our Mastiff with Counter-IED rollers, a formidable beast of a vehicle. My team and I have lots of experience of clearing routes and making convoys safe. It makes me really proud to be able to do this and it also feels quite a big responsibility knowing that other people's safety is in my hands.

Breakfast had been at some crazy time (about 0200) so we cracked open our plastic pot of noodles that we shared around after about 1 hour on the road. Bit spicy but just the way we like it.

The journey to Showal was 3.5 hours long and after about 2 hours my driver shouted 'Stop!' The vehicle in front of us had spotted an IED. My team got out the Mastiff to assess the danger and the decision was made to divert the convoy on another route. It's our business to create by-pass routes and provide that safe passage. Was I nervous? Well actually not. Though it sounds big-headed, I don't get nervous easily but I am cautious and careful.

And so the convoy reached Showal on time. We were greeted by the Engineers who were in a hurry to see us and in a bigger hurry to build the patrol base.

⬔ Dealing with death is our job

2 March 2010

Trooper Pete Sheppard, BRF

It was a weird day weather-wise. It has been nice and hot for the past few days and then overnight there was a lot of thunder and lightning lighting up the sky. It was shortly followed up by a large outburst of heavy rain/hail stones. It only lasted a couple of hours and in the morning the weather has gone back to normal again with clear blue skies.

Was speaking to one of the lads who was in Foxy's troop and he was saying how it hasn't even sunk in yet what had happened. He then said it probably will soon though. I think that is generally the same feeling across most of us. It's crazy to think that one minute someone is there, and the next he's not. But this is what we sign up to do and it is our job.

The local children are jumping into the small canal near us to cool down. They seem oblivious to our presence and are enjoying themselves, somersaulting into the cool water. One of the interpreters joined in and was jumping in as well, while we just observed.

The lads were talking about getting to Cyprus. We all are looking forward to coming home now. Just counting the days down still. Everyday is just one closer to coming home. Can't wait.

◥ A slightly better place

3 March 2010

Flight Sergeant Paul Groombridge, Military Stabilisation

Support Team, RAF Regiment

As my tour comes to an end, I'm able to reflect on probably one of the most rewarding and diverse jobs in Helmand. Being a member of the Military Stabilisation Support Team (MSST) has enabled me to access virtually every element within both the civil and military communities, where one day I may be speaking to the Minister of Education in order to build a school, and the next day patrolling the Green Zone with members of the French Foreign Legion mentoring the Afghan National Army.

The MSST is an element of the Provincial Reconstruction Team (PRT) that exists to extend the reach of civilian District Stabilisation Advisers (DSTABAD) to operate across areas of Helmand that are not safe to civilians.

Teams consist of around four individuals that are responsible primarily for assisting long-term stabilisation by identifying

Flight Sergeant Paul Groombridge, RAF Regiment, with Major Ed Hill at a Shura. [Picture: Major Paul Smyth]

projects and programmes that assist communities to develop both socially and economically. They also provide the DSTABAD with a deployable asset to assist and advise military commanders during operations where there is considerable disruption to communities in a 'Hot Stabilisation' role.

As a member of the RAF Regiment I was well equipped for the voluntary 6-month tour of duty with the joint service MSST, which was preceded by a 3-month period of training. After working closely with the Queen's Company of the Grenadier Guards for 5 months north of Lashkar Gah, I was redeployed and attached to B Company, 1 Royal Welsh, in preparation of Op Moshtarak which has been one of the largest operations to take place in Helmand since British forces arrived in theatre.

Following a dawn helicopter insertion into the former Taliban stronghold of Shaheed, my first task was to liaise with the owners of compounds that had been occupied by ANA and

ISAF troops. This is probably one of the most difficult jobs, knowing how I would feel if told that I had to leave my home and land, in some cases permanently, so that it could be turned into a patrol base. In the case of all but one compound, the owners would be able to return within a week or two and, after being given an assistance payment and a letter enabling them to claim rent, were content with the temporary situation.

Since the initial phase of Moshtarak, regular patrols with both ANA and ISAF have dominated my days in order to learn the area and gain an understanding of the community's needs so that I can assist it with its development, which will include the provision of education. Shuras, which involve a gathering of village elders, are an integral component of the stabilisation process and enable me to talk to the key leaders of the village, passing information and listening to their concerns.

It has been a demanding tour, sometimes frustrating, always challenging, but I hope that I've left Afghanistan a slightly better place than when I arrived in September last year.

⚫ Downtime sparks discussion

3 March 2010

Trooper Pete Sheppard, BRF

It was yet another quiet day for the BRF. The troops went out through the night last night on routine patrols to observe any enemy activity. Upon returning to our leaguer they took the opportunity to catch up on much-deserved rest.

A few of the guys have been talking amongst each other, expressing their desire not to come back out here to Afghanistan. Some of the lads want to just leave the Army altogether. I can appreciate the stress it puts the lads under with regards to their wife and children if they have any back at home. For me, though, the military seems to be the right career.

It has been quite cloudy today, not as warm as recent days, which I hope is just a temporary thing. However, the nice cool breeze is refreshing.

A couple of vehicles went and got some food resupplies yesterday. Included in this were American rations, water, an assortment of chocolate bars and a load of sweets sent through from the welfare packs. We all really appreciate these.

A couple of our troops went out on a patrol about 1600 and received some small arms fire. They returned fire as trained and took cover. We were getting a lot of insurgent chatter over their radios, saying that they could see us and were going to start firing again. But nothing further came from this.

The insurgent took cover in a compound and we waited for our air assets to try and positively ID him with a weapon. We couldn't see anything so they withdrew. Once back at our location, our air assets picked up two assessed insurgents with one believed to be carrying a weapon of some sort across his back. So we sent another patrol out to follow these guys up. Once the patrol had eyes on the two insurgents we saw them walk away and could not do anything about it. Maybe a busy night for us tonight.

Tim from the Fire Support Team dropped two packs of noodles that he was cooking. He got those from a welfare pack. He is not a happy man.

◪ Nightshift

3 March 2010

Corporal Steph Hodgson, Emergency Ward Nurse at Camp Bastion Field Hospital

Whist writing this blog there is pandemonium going on behind me, banging, raised voices, some in anger ... no, there isn't a mass trauma situation going on, it's Team Alpha playing cards on a nightshift! Thankfully nights are usually calm (you never actually say 'quiet' as that only means trouble!!)

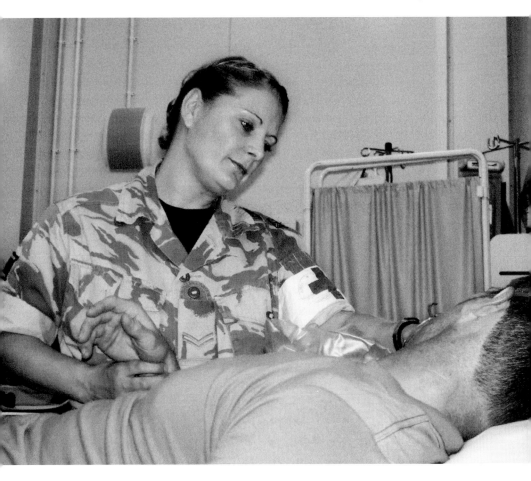

My name is Corporal Steph Hodgson and I am a nurse working in the Emergency Department of Camp Bastion. My day job is working for the NHS as a Sister in trauma plastics back in Blighty, but as I am in the Territorial Army (TA), I have been deployed to Afghanistan. This is my second tour. Now I have been asked to blog a week of my life in Afghan, and as I have never blogged a week in my life anywhere, this is going to be ... interesting for me! But looking on the bright side, I am a woman, so I can talk forever.

I have been attached to 205 (Scottish) Field Hospital and, as I am English, I thought that I may need an interpreter to understand the Scots, let alone the Afghans, but they are a professional and kind bunch and ignore my poor attempts at a Scottish accent. I am working with a mixed bunch of

Corporal Steph Hodgson with a patient at Camp Bastion.

regular and TA soldiers, and a first for me: I am working with the Americans!

This is a Joint Forces and Multi National run hospital, so we work closely together to provide the best care for our men and women of all nationalities. The accent isn't so much of a problem this time, but some of the terminology can be a little ... confusing, such as 'fanny bag', that's bum bag to us, and to be honest the rest is unprintable. Oh and someone must have mentioned the Q word as we've just been given notice that we have two Cat A's coming in by helicopter (now I'm going to bore you with the actual work bit). The estimated time of arrival (ETA) is 0130 hrs.

We have a priority system that all incoming patients are given on the seriousness of their injuries. This is called a 'nine liner'. Cat A is life threatening and needs immediate treatment, Cat B is injured or ill but stable and Cat C is what we call 'walking wounded'.

We are expecting a gunshot wound (GSW) to the abdomen, and GSW to the left leg. The trauma team has been alerted, which includes an anaesthetist, specialist surgeons, doctors and, of course, us nurses and medics. I just need to go and help my mates set up the bays ready to receive the patients and then I will come back after we have cared for the causalities.

Right, it's now 0323 hrs and we've spent the last hour and a half dealing with both the Cat As and a Cat B ... they're like buses, none for hours then three come all at once!!! They all are quite stable now and tucked up in bed, as they're not as seriously injured as first thought. This often happens, the nine liner does not always match the patients' actual trauma, hence why we've renamed it the nine liar! You never know exactly what's coming through the door! That's what makes this job so challenging.

0500 hrs trauma call, another Cat A ...

⬐ Waiting to go out on bomb patrol

4 March 2010

Trooper Pete Sheppard, BRF

Reveille was at 0600 this morning. I did not sleep well at all.

We woke up and the first thing we did was pack all of our kit away. This included all of the radio masts and laptops we use for file transfers. I was due to go out on patrol very soon, so I was checking last bits of kit. Once we had done this we threw some scoff in the BV (boiling vessel) to heat up and eat shortly.

The previous day, 3 Troop (Foxy used to be in this one) went back to Bastion for a larger service there. They returned for first light this morning with a small number of cold pizzas, which they had bought the previous night at Pizza Hut. That was awesome!

At 0700 the patrol that I was in set off to a compound that we are taking over for a few days. We are pushing closer towards the enemy's positions. We do not just rock up and move the locals out; we actually pay them money like compensation for us moving in.

We gave them a couple of hours to remove any of their belongings and then we moved into the compound. This patrol only had about eight British and about nine ATF (it was not the whole BRF yet).

A few hours later the Jackals and Coyotes started to arrive. We had to make a small bridge so that the vehicles could cross the irrigation ditches, but within a couple of hours everyone was in.

Once in this compound, we positioned all of the vehicles facing rearwards, set up the radios, sorted our kit out and got some hot food on the go. It has been quite hot today so we have all been drinking a lot of water.

Again, some of the guys keep saying how they are breaking and really cannot wait to get home. The support everyone gives us is brilliant and I can say that we are all grateful for this.

It is just getting dark now, been a long day. Everyone is up at ridiculous o'clock, as the troops are going out on big clearance patrols. It is straight to bed for the majority of people now. Need all the rest we can get for tomorrow.

◤ Contact at Loy Doreh

4 March 2010

Squadron Leader Dee Taylor, RAF, Media Ops

Fire Support, 1 Royal Welsh, had a patrol to undertake in the afternoon. Within 20 minutes of leaving Checkpoint Bennett (a new CP established to provide security along Route 603), the 30-man patrol came under fire from the Taliban. It was a feisty skirmish from the insurgents, with a sustained small fire arms attack.

In the Ops Room, map pins were rapidly pushed into a grey map showing the positions of the three platoons and suspected insurgent position. Captain Frankie Taylor, the second in command of the Company, was calmly questioning the two radio operators to establish where the contacts were coming from. But no sooner had the ground picture been established, than the Taliban melted away. There had been lots of shouting heard over the radio, as soldiers carried out tried and tested drills. There had been no reports of casualties.

Frankie and the Ops Team dutifully reported the incident to HQ and the rear party. Soon after, the commanding officer of the Royal Welsh, Lieutenant Colonel Nick Lock, landed at the checkpoint for a planned visit to meet the Fire Support Team both in the compound and on patrol. Having done a quick tour of the compound, he was out on the ground to join up with the patrol.

It was only to be 20 minutes later that the crack of gunfire could be heard from the compound. The crack turned into a vicious exchange of shots, with each side aggressively laying down fire. The radio operators could hear the excited and charged voices of the platoon commanders panting out positions and updates. Two of the Afghan soldiers had been wounded.

The compound gates were rapidly opened. However, it was not the wounded but the commanding officer who came into the compound. 'We missed the action by about 2 minutes'; there was a tinge of regret in his voice. Frankie was able to brief Lieutenant Colonel Nick Lock that both casualties were walking wounded; one had been shot in the foot, whilst the other had sustained shrapnel wounds to his right leg and arm. The two combat medics had rushed to their aid patching up both soldiers deftly and the platoon quickly got them out of harm's way. Brought in by Jackal vehicle, the two casualties were very quickly bandaged and made comfortable; Corporal

Skills combat medics tend to the wounded Afghan warriors. [Picture: Squadron Leader Dee Taylor]

157

Raphael Gbedebu and Private Jason Edwardson, the combat medics, saw to that.

'Give these guys some room,' shouted Corporal Gbedebu, as concerned Afghan comrades gathered around the injured men. His tone of voice needed no translation. The two medics then set about treating their wounds gently but quickly. Both soldiers were very much aware of their injuries but had been reassured by the medics that they would be patched up and that their injuries were 'very manageable'.

Frankie put in the 'nine-liner' report on the triage state of the casualties and requested that a helicopter casevac the wounded soldiers back to Camp Bastion. He was as thorough in his reporting as he was deft. Over the net, HQ acknowledged the request. 'Boys,' said Frankie in a beguiling Welsh lilt, 'let's get these casualties to the helicopter site; medics say they can walk – job done.' Praise doesn't come higher than that in Fire Support Company. 'Well not for us old and bolds,' said Frankie.

◥ A very close shave

8 March 2010

Rifleman James McKie, Recce Platoon, 3 RIFLES

[Rifleman James McKie was under fire from three directions in Sangin when the hand grenade hit his platoon commander and landed at his feet. He picked it up and threw it back in an attempt to save his colleagues.]

The fire was disciplined and accurate. I managed to spot one of the firing points and I engaged with my General Purpose Machine Gun (GPMG) to suppress the enemy. After a few minutes they stopped firing and we continued observing to the east. It must have been no more than five minutes and then I heard what sounded like a mini flare come from our right, where I knew there were none of our guys, so I thought this was really unusual. It was actually the fly-off lever of a grenade that had been thrown from the alleyway below.

Rifleman James McKie.

We were in a high position on a compound roof. There was no way you could throw yourself off and not get injured, so I made a decision to pick up the grenade and throw it off the roof. And I threw it quite deliberately. My first thought was, I hope this doesn't hurt too much. That and I've really only got one chance to do this. If it fails, either way, doing nothing, I'm going to get the same amount of hurt. So I picked it up and threw it off the roof.

I tried to throw it properly, to clear the roof. I didn't want to do it half-arsed and have them throw it back at us or anything like that. I remember thinking that if I didn't pull this off, it was going to hurt. But at that stage I was pretty much committed.

My platoon has taken a lot of casualties. I really didn't want to see anyone else get hurt. So I committed to that course of action. It was dropping down into the alleyway before it detonated. As I continued to watch it, as you are trained to, I received fragmentation in my face and right arm. Because of the way Captain Kerr was positioned, he got a larger piece of fragmentation in his left leg, but otherwise no one else was seriously hurt.

In retrospect, people keep telling me how brave I am, which I'm slightly embarrassed about. I'd like to think that anyone in that situation would have done the same or something similar, because you can't just sit there and let yourself or other people get hurt. I don't feel particularly brave. I thought: I have to do this to survive. Not just for myself but for the guys around me as well. I'm not expecting anything from them, I don't want any thanks from them. I just don't want them to get hurt.

⧉ Fighting alongside the Afghan Army and Police

8 March 2010

Major Paul Smyth, RIFLES, Media Ops

The patrol started off just like any other from Patrol Base Shaheed (2.5km north-east of Showal). The Afghan National Army and Afghan National Police were in the lead as they are for most of the patrols in the area. As usual, they had with them a handful of British soldiers from the 1st Battalion The Royal Welsh, and me, there to offer support if needed.

Patrol Base Shaheed was set up following Operation Moshtarak, which took place just over three weeks ago. It was the largest air assault in Helmand since the campaign started in 2001.

We were in the Green Zone and out to dominate the ground taken during the operation.

An hour into the patrol the tranquillity was shattered just after the Afghan Security Forces left a compound where

they had been talking to village elders. Insurgents opened up on the rear of the patrol from a few hundred metres away using neighbouring compounds for cover. We took cover in an irrigation ditch, observing the insurgents' movements and returning fire.

Using the Afghans to suppress the insurgents, we moved location to join up with the ANA and ANP commanders. While the Afghans kept the insurgents pinned down, the Brit patrol commander, Lieutenant Adam Libby, called in surveillance aircraft to monitor the insurgents' movements, as well as a show of force.

Within minutes, a US fast jet was flying in within a few hundred feet of the ground, dropping flares to send out a very clear message to the insurgents that the patrol on the ground had some very significant firepower to call on if needed.

A combined patrol of Afghan National Army, Afghan National Police and a small contingent of Brits at the back. [Picture: Major Paul Smyth]

An Afghan National Policeman puts down some covering fire. [Picture: Major Paul Smyth]

The key to this firefight was to use just the right amount of force to suppress the insurgents and minimise damage to the area. All around us farmers and their families were tending to their crops and going about their day as usual. With aircraft up in the sky monitoring the situation, we headed back to base knowing that the insurgents' every move was being tracked. We did well today, pushing back the insurgents and sending them a pretty clear message that they are not welcome here in Shaheed.

◥ Succumbing to the idea of staying longer

10 March 2010

Trooper Pete Sheppard, BRF

This morning we found out that the brigade want to extend our time on the ground. There were mixed feelings about this.

On the whole, though, it's a good thing as it just makes the time we have left on the ground go quicker. We are also going to be going into Lashkar Gah at some point for 12 hours so we can have a shower, use a proper toilet, get some clothes washed, eat some hot food and get some supplies from the shop there. The food there is immense.

We heard across the radio a warning of a controlled explosion this morning from someone else. We passed round our guy's notice of the warning. Not everyone heard the warning.

One of the guys came over to me after the explosion and told me that he and the guys were stood around laughing and joking when the bang went off. We had troops out working on a culvert but as it came from that general direction they just all went quiet and looked at each other thinking the worst. I was told you could hear a pin drop. They then heard that it was a controlled explosion and there was a big sigh of relief.

Today we've been building a culvert 500m down the road for the locals. They seem to really appreciate this and it is good for us to help win the support from them.

It's been hard work for the troops, though, as it has been 26 degrees today with no wind.

Some of the guys have made makeshift weights to use when back at the compound. Me and Dave used the outdoor makeshift gym earlier and are both feeling the aches and pains from it now. It's amazing how much strength you actually lose from not doing any weights or press-ups for so long.

Everyone is succumbing to the idea of being extended longer and morale is slowly creeping back up.

The days are going quite quickly, so before too long we'll be back at Bastion handing our kit over to the next BRF.

◪ Well-earned rest in Afghanistan

11 March 2010

Trooper Pete Sheppard, BRF

We have spent the last couple of days in a really well-equipped main base close by. We went there to replenish our water, fuel and rations and also to have a shower, wash our clothes and eat some hot food.

We managed to get some more clothing issued to us, which was handy because the days living in the field had started to take their toll on some of the guys' kit.

This also gave us the opportunity to ring home, go on the Internet and buy some of those little niceties from the shop there before deploying back to our base.

Today, at 0815, I went out as part of a small patrol made up of some guys in Squadron Headquarters (SHQ) to move a bridge crossing a canal. When I say a bridge, it's just two ladders strapped together to increase the length across the canal, but you still get wet just over your boots. We moved this 'bridge' about 100m further down a track and dug steps into the steep banks of the canal to make it easier to cross. We were back at the compound within an hour.

The locals have asked us to build a permanent bridge crossing the canal for them, so I took some pictures of the proposed bridging site to send up to higher headquarters to decide.

At about 0830, the rest of the squadron went out on a patrol. They went out for about seven hours, clearing through the small groups of compounds and interacting with the locals. The local atmospherics were good, and the troops didn't encounter any trouble.

They returned at 1430. Some of the guys from SHQ were stood at the entrance to the compound with bottles of water to give out to the lads as they came in.

It has been hot today; AJ measured the temperature to be 27.5 degrees Celsius! You can appreciate how hard it is for the troops having to patrol and run around with their body armour, helmets, ammo and bags on in that kind of heat.

Once everyone was in, they chilled out and stripped off their kit, and got some well-earned rest.

It's been confirmed that our time on the ground has been extended yet again. When our boss was telling us, he said that this was good, because this means that we actually are eventually coming off the ground. Everyone had a laugh at that.

⟡ DIY SOS – more like 'Extreme Building'

11 March 2010

Corporal 'AD' Adrian Dixon, 28 Section Engineering Support Group

It's a bit like being Nick Knowles from DIY SOS. But instead of sorting out a dilapidated bathroom in 24 hours, we have to make an all-singing, all-dancing patrol base here in Showal, Nad-e-Ali, in less than 3 weeks. This is not an easy task when you have to put in a checkpoint first to protect the area. So you have to turn infantryman to make sure there is no IED threat, put your builders on sentry duty and then put in the basics of any checkpoint – sangars, firing points, chicanes and search bays.

Now the patrol base we are building required a Medium Girder Bridge to bridge the gap over a small irrigation channel. It was about a 5–6 metre gap, and without the bridge, no building supplies or stores could be brought in by the 60-vehicle Combat Logistics Patrol. It also had to be sturdy enough to take some significant weight from containerized lorries. We started building it at 0530 and it took us a day to complete.

We are on a tight timescale of no longer than 3 weeks to make a complete patrol base that will house Afghan soldiers

Corporal 'AD'
Adrian Dixon.

and coalition troops. We are working in partnership with ANA engineers, but it is a challenge as site foreman to relay building instructions in Pashtu! I find hand gestures work much better – oh, and use of an interpreter. We are working 18- to 20-hour shifts until the base is built, with only 6 hours off to rest for each person.

We did have some dramas when our plant broke which fills aggregate into the Hesco security bins. Hesco are flat-pack frames that we fill with earth to make thick compound wall very quickly. However, we reverted to type one spade and filled the bins in by hand. The only thing then that stopped the plan was a sandstorm that raged on for 7 hours. However, we are on schedule and I'm very proud of what our lads have achieved.

◥ Close Air Support

12 March 2010

Flight Lieutenant Ben 'Goody' Goodwin, GR4 Tornado Pilot

9 Squadron, Kandahar Airfield

Operation Moshtarak was fairly anti-climactic for the GR4s. It was undoubtedly exciting to be involved in the build-up, as we all planned for the worst and hoped for the best. The Close Air Support (CAS) preparation we do at home focuses on kinetics, understanding the weapons, how to use them in difficult circumstances to achieve the precise results we aim

Flight Lieutenant Ben 'Goody' Goodwin with his Tornado GR4.

for. It's training for the 'worst' scenario – everyone being shot at, enemy difficult to spot, friendlies close by.

I find the hardest part of CAS is interpreting the situation correctly and concentrating through very long periods of boredom. Every event is different; each presents its own unique challenges. To generate such a training scenario is almost impossible, so we rely on experience and flexibility.

The challenges in Moshtarak, as they are mostly in theatre, were staying focused during long sorties operating in busy airspace not designed for only fast air's requirements. Covering patrols really showed just how far 12,000 feet can be, us warm in our cockpit, less than ten minutes flying time from Kandahar, watching soldiers walk down the streets and through the compounds, right in the thick of it.

I remember one moment, where a patrol moved through a slim doorway into a compound they had asked us to survey. We'd reported suspicious activity including dickers and possible weapons. But in they went to the courtyard and chatted to the locals.

In the end, the GR4s never had to employ any weapons in support of the operation, and perhaps the biggest contribution we made was through our Reconnaissance Airborne Pod for Tornado, otherwise known as RAPTOR, which provided imagery of the battle space, searching for IEDs and surveying landing zones. Above Marjeh we hoped that our noise was signature enough to deter some attacks, and the smoothness of the operation suggests that this might be in some small way true.

◩ The uncertainty of war

14 March 2010

Trooper Pete Sheppard, BRF

Today we got up for 0700. It was already quite warm so we knew it was going to be a hot day. The first patrols left our location at 0900 on foot in order to secure a vehicle checkpoint (VCP) and interact with locals.

At 1050 another one of our troops got airlifted by helicopter 4km away. The plan was for the guys at the VCP to draw the insurgents out to them and then the guys dropped off by the helicopter could cut them off. Simultaneous to this, another patrol left our location by foot as a back-up, in case something happened. Strangely nothing happened.

The insurgents were very quiet all day, maybe due to the losses they received yesterday. There were a few suspicious locals but nothing came of this. The patrols returned early afternoon when the sun was in its prime.

The thing with this place is you never know what the day's going to bring. You can prepare yourself for a big engagement – and we all convince ourselves it's going happen – and the day goes off without a whisper. And other days – routine days when it should be quiet – all hell breaks loose.

The weather has increased by over five degrees this week. Lads are returning off these patrols dripping in sweat. They look exhausted – but they continuously soldier on and are constantly ready to get called out again – ready for those unexpected days.

Still getting bitten, but the antihistamine cream is helping. Slowly. One day closer to home.

◥ A huge learning experience

14 March 2010

Corporal Simon Smith, D Company, 1 Royal Welsh

I am a multiple (a multiple is made up to 12) commander with 10 Platoon, D Company. My working pattern currently finds me located in the main company patrol base doing two days' guard followed by two days' patrolling.

Our patrols have ranged from a Company-sized operation of 70 Afghan National Army plus 40 International Security and Assistance Force (ISAF) soldiers to multiple sized patrols for security.

For the first 14 days I had a platoon that was composed of 15 ISAF and 15 ANA living in a single, small compound. This was a huge learning experience as we were two different cultures in a very small compound and there was just the one interpreter enabling us to talk to each other. We used that compound to mount joint patrols in the area.

Whilst on patrol we look to reassure the locals that we are here to provide security. We seek out projects that will improve the area and yesterday we took books to a mosque that teaches 100 children. Today we will focus on route clearance.

When we first conducted a route clearance we tackled an area that was a crossroads where the Taliban were running an illegal checkpoint. It had Taliban flags flying from a tree.

There was even a sign that read: To all Muslim people in our country the Taliban are laying bombs in this area at night, stay away from this area. We cleared the route, then the ANA changed the flag to an Afghan flag, watched by the people in the local area. It was a good start to Operation Moshtarak.

Last night 11 Platoon found an IED. This morning we went out and they handed over the task of over-watch of the area to us and we checked a nearby compound. The more we searched the compound, the more IED component parts we found, from battery packs to explosives.

We had kept an eye on the man who owned the compound whilst this was going on and, once we'd finished searching, the ANA that we were working with went and arrested him. Further tests confirmed that he had been handling explosives. Today has been a good day for us, as it means less IEDs are available to the insurgents.

Corporal Simon Smith briefs his patrol before heading out.

I am particularly proud of my multiple as it is newly formed; not one of my soldiers has been in the Army longer than a year. They have all stepped up to the mark and remained professional throughout. We have managed to gather a lot of intelligence through speaking to locals and working closely with the ANA and ANP. I think this is in part due to our having done so much Pre-Deployment Training before coming out to Helmand.

Whatever the reason, their professionalism and positive attitude has enabled us to have successful days like today.

◱ Some people ...

21 March 2010

Corporal Dave Morrison, Information Co-ordinator,

Royal Air Force Police

I am asked from time to time to attend local events in villages around Camp Bastion to help out with security and find out what concerns the locals may have. We have got a large event on, with a good crowd gathered to visit a medical clinic. I have to get to work straight away because some of the locals have arrived early.

It's a really good sign that so many people have showed up even before the security forces from the Afghan National Army and ISAF have pitched up; guess the radio works for local Afghan stations as well as BFBS does for us. Anyway, it's a case of setting up our cam netting and making a shady area to chat to locals in. Who wants to be talking outside in 33 degrees if it can be helped?

Corporal Dave Morrison chats to a local Afghan boy. [Picture: Squadron Leader Dee Taylor]

Since my Pashtu is pretty poor to say the least, I have Mohammad Ali the interpreter to help translate my conversations. Well, he says his name is Mohammad Ali ... I enjoy the challenge of adapting my rapport as some people just want to be business like when we talk, whilst others like to sit down and chat, and just a few like to jump up and down!

I meet with a variety of local Afghan men with ages ranging from 16 to 60, probably seeing nearly forty. Most are local farmers who by and large are tending wheat crops. They nearly all are saying that the wheat price is pretty good at the moment and seem upbeat on prices they are getting. But like most farmers, they could probably do with a bit more.

There are a couple of people whose jobs are more to do with looking after farm machinery and general maintenance. I asked these guys how they are finding using the solar-powered water purifier that was installed about a month ago. They said that it was a bit strange at first and people were quite suspicious of it. But now they have got used to it and it helps a lot. Most of the local villagers are still a little unsure exactly how it runs, but at least there are a couple of people now who are getting confident with the day-to-day running of the kit.

◪ A quiet day turned busy

24 March 2010

Colour Sergeant Damo Hudson, Forward Air Controller (FAC),

D Company, 1 Royal Welsh

I have been the FAC for D Company, 1 Royal Welsh, since the start of their tour. My role is to advise the Company commander on the assets available for Close Air Support (CAS). I also direct Intelligence, Surveillance, Target Acquisition and Reconnaissance (ISTAR) assets to where he requires them, and interpret the images that are relayed back to me via the downlink. In addition, I guide the helicopters in to helicopter landing sites (HLSs) when the Company is being resupplied or we have people leaving or joining us.

This morning I woke up and checked what air (ISTAR or CAS) assets I had been allocated. The Company commander then gave me my tasks for the day. Today, I am looking for signs or movement that would indicate IED placements on one of the roads going into the village. So I settled at my desk in the Ops Room, hoping for a quiet day.

Colour Sergeant
Damo Hudson.

My job is mostly reactive so a quiet day is a good day. The Ops Room has been set up in one of the rooms in the compound we are operating from and currently houses the HQ elements of 1 Royal Welsh and number 1 Company of 1/3/201 Kandak and their French mentors.

A couple of hours into the start of the day there was an almighty explosion; one of our Mastiffs had been hit whilst going out to pick up some Engineers from a checkpoint (CP).

Thus my quiet day turned busy. I radioed back to our headquarter element in Camp Bastion for an ISTAR asset and I was given an Unmanned Aerial Vehicle (UAV) to provide over-watch of the area. I was able to use this to provide protection to our lads who were dealing with the incident outside the compound.

After the area was checked for further IEDs, I tracked the recovery of the vehicle back to our compound. Again, my role was to provide over-watch in order to protect our guys during the process. I also used the UAV to scan the rest of the route for signs of further IEDs.

Finally, I used the UAV to provide security for a funeral procession that passed along the route later that day which the ANA and ANP attended. We had a fear that the IED attack might be followed up by small arms fire, or worse, and so we kept the UAV on task to ensure that the funeral could take place in relative safety.

As the day ended, I had a short rest before putting in requests for assets required over the next few days and starting my night shift of maintaining over-watch over the areas requested by the commanding officer.

In order to do this job I have been attached to 1 Royal Horse Artillery who are based in Tidworth. I will hold the post of FAC for two years before returning to The Royal Welsh. This job is very different to what I have done before and I have enjoyed it.

Developing basic Pashtu

28 March 2010

Colour Sergeant Johns, Non Kinetic Effects Team, 1 Royal Welsh

I am part of the D Company Non Kinetic Effects Team, 1 Royal Welsh. I am attached to D Company and have been based with their HQ element since Operation Moshtarak started in the western Babaji area.

During Operation Moshtarak I have been working alongside Sergeant Major Anthony MacGann, who is a member of the Military Stabilisation and Support Team (MSST). Our roles vary from providing support to the local population and aiding with reconstruction, to dealing with Psychological Operations (Psy Ops), which make use of the sound commander, a form of loudspeaker.

Colour Sergeant
Johns. [Picture:
Major Paul Smyth]

On the ground I may use the sound commander to let the local
population know of upcoming Shuras, to encourage people
to meet their District Community Council representative, to
let them know we can provide emergency medical treatment
and to advertise for skilled workers in order to employ them in
local reconstruction and development projects.

On a day-to-day basis we deal with walk-ins which vary
from people asking for compensation for damaged property
to requests for emergency medical assistance. The most
common medical complaint we see is scalding for children
and infections from cuts for adults. We also had one child who
came in who had been shot in the shoulder some weeks back

(prior to the troops' arrival to the area). We checked the wound and the doctor gave him exercises to do to strengthen it and prevent the muscles from withering away.

My basic Pashtu is developing. Prior to deployment I took part in a five-day course designed to enable us to issue orders to locals when on VCPs and conducting searches. Since arriving in Nad-e-Ali, I have used greetings and developed my general conversational skills with the children.

I work with the MSST in organising Shuras which are then run by the ANA. We have bought carpets, glasses and teapots for the chai in order to be able to host the locals properly. Before each Shura we buy fresh chai and cakes. These are all bought from the local bazaar. If people are staying for lunch then we will serve fat-tailed sheep, a delicacy that is named from the local sheep which have fatty bottoms!

The fat is fried and is a bit like crackling. It is cooked, along with the meat, with potatoes and red onions by the ANA and served with rice. It is not heavily spiced, is quite greasy, but tastes good and it is always a treat to eat fresh food. The largest Shura organised at this location so far has been for over 80 people.

The local bazaar has increased in trade due to the improved security in the area and because it is serving the newly arrived ANA and ANP in the area. We visit the bazaar too; every Friday we buy potatoes which we then use to cook chips. This is the first time I have worked as a member of the Non Kinetic Effects Team. Though it can take time for the positive effects of our work to show, it is a highly rewarding job.

⧨ Once the dust settled

29 March 2010

Lieutenant Mark Lewis, 10 Platoon Commander, D Company,

1 Royal Welsh

I am a platoon commander for D Company and am currently based with Company Headquarters in a compound in Loy Adehra. We have been there since the start of Operation Moshtarak.

Our first two weeks here consisted of meeting and greeting the locals we met on patrols and explaining that we are in the area in order to provide enduring security as part of combined force operations. With us in Loy Adehra we have 1 Company

Lieutenant Mark Lewis tries out some new transport.

from 1/3/201 Kandak of the Afghan National Army, with their French mentors and 50 Afghan National Police.

We also held Shuras at our compound led by the ANA. This work paid off, with people gaining the confidence to tend their fields and attend the twice-weekly bazaar; we had over 1,000 people turn up at the last bazaar.

However, during this last week insurgent activity has started to pick up. Firstly, we had a failed IED strike on one of the main routes through the village. Shortly after this we conducted patrols around the area and discovered an IED in one of the fields near our compound.

We followed this up with a compound search and discovered IED component parts that matched that of the device. From this we, along with the ANA, were then able to detain one of the insurgents and further questioning and tests confirmed he had been handling explosives. During questioning I was able to ascertain that he was involved with the IEDs and we were able to send him back to Bastion to be questioned further.

Yesterday, we were on a routine patrol through a local village and my vehicle was involved in an IED strike. A pressure pad IED with approximately 50kg of explosive lifted the Mastiff across the narrow street. The Mastiff did what it was designed to do and took the brunt of the explosion.

I was top cover at the time and blown out of the turret, but stopped from landing in the nearby field by the cam net. Once the dust settled I could hear the lads in the cabin moaning and yelling. I dropped down fearing the worst, not knowing what I would see next. Thankfully both lads were ok, with only minor back and leg injuries. The next day we were straight back out on another patrol.

To break the monotony of rations, once a week we have fried sausages and homemade chips from potatoes bought in the bazaar.

◪ It's a big contract to the day job

31 March 2010

Lance Corporal Katie Guntrip, 47 Air Dispatch (AD)

I am a TA soldier on my first operational tour, currently deployed on a three-month detachment with 47 Air Dispatch (AD) based in Kandahar. We are a crew of six Air Dispatchers with seven local employees assigned to work with us.

The Air Dispatch role is used to supply vital stores, equipment, rations and water to ground troops who may be unable to be resupplied by road or who require an urgent resupply. The day-to-day job involves rigging the equipment, aircraft loading

Lance Corporal Katie Guntrip prepares for an Air Dispatch mission.

and flying on the air drop sorties. There are also other tasks that are completed, such as vehicle and store management, which are crucial to support our work. We work very closely with the RAF C130 Hercules crews and together we resupply any military unit or service on the ground.

The tour so far has been a relatively busy one. On top of our normal workload we were required to support Op Moshtarak by preparing 110 containers ready for air drop over a 10-day period, working around 14 to 16 hours a day. The crew was on 24-hour standby over the course of the operation if required.

Our role in the operation was to allow the ground troops to maintain momentum by resupplying with rations, fuel, water and ammunition. This was a large amount of work to be completed to support multinational forces from France, Estonia, Afghanistan, as well as British ground troops. Our hard work didn't go unnoticed as the Det later received an Air Commodore's Commendation for our efforts on the Op.

Our regular taskings have also meant us air dropping to FOBs and patrol bases. I have flown on one sortie which was a really good experience, very different from the training sorties that I fly at weekends, mainly because we fly at night, observing through the doors wearing night vision goggles, body armour and with our weapons.

On a personal note, I have found my time here very rewarding and feel that as a crew we have worked well and proven to a large audience that we can react quickly and achieve a great deal in a short space of time – even if that meant a 24-hour working day, which has happened on more than one occasion on our tour!

It is a big contrast to my normal civilian desk job, but will look back on my time here with a sense of achievement and pleased that we had the opportunity to be involved in the Op, proving that our role, although relatively small, can be a key part of resupply missions.

⟩ Tears and tributes to a 'good guy'

6 April 2010

Trooper Pete Sheppard, BRF

They say a watched kettle never boils. You could also say that time never moves slower than when you are in Camp Bastion just waiting to go home.

The Brigade Reconnaissance Force came back into Bastion on 26 March having completed their final op. I wish I could say there was a real end of term atmosphere, that there were big smiles all round. Instead, there was just the awful realisation that whether you are on your first day, or your last – the last day as it turns out – your luck can still run out.

We were in the area north of Five Ways Junction, a major meeting of roads that lead to Marjah, Lashkar Gah and places like that. We had sent a recce party forward to liaise with the Americans because we were passing through their area. We pushed through and set ourselves up in a leaguer – long lines of vehicles – in the middle of open ground but surrounded by poppy fields and mud compounds.

The next day was spent pushing out patrols and clearing compounds. Nothing much happened that day and when the patrols returned we got the orders from higher to return to Bastion. We were to take part in a 36-hour op in the Sangin area, leaving 25 March.

Everyone was chuffed about that – returning to Bastion is a chance to shower, wash clothes and eat hot, fresh food.

So we started to move back into Bastion on the night of 22 March. We drove to The Household Cavalry Regiment checkpoint and waited for last light. We took a very long route back – you can't afford to set patterns out here.

As we were coming through Gereshk, right in the centre, we got small arms fire. It's the first time we've come under contact in Gereshk that I know of.

It was pitch black. We have kit allowing us to drive at night, but it's tiring using it for a long time. We crossed the bridge and there were rounds flinging right in front of us, literally 2m in front of my face. You could see the individual tracer winging past.

We swore a bit but just kept pushing on, foot down. None of us fired back, it was just too risky in case we hit an innocent civilian.

As we were coming out of Gereshk on Highway 1 we saw lots of fire and illumination shells in the distance. Apparently, one of the Afghan National Police checkpoints was getting contacted, so we stopped there, waited half an hour or so to try and suss out what was happening and then carried on to Bastion.

We had been out of Bastion for several weeks by this point and everyone just wanted to get back in, shower and eat. People had headaches from the long hard drive.

They've put a new gate in with increased security and everyone was getting more and more pissed off as the guards insisted on checking every one of our vehicles and all the individuals inside. We were clearly British, wearing British uniform and driving British vehicles. Our sense of humour evaporated at this point.

Once we were in, we locked our weapons away and just about the whole squadron headed for Pizza Hut and from there straight to bed.

The 23rd and 24th was spent in camp sorting out personal kit and prepping for the op. I was told that I was to stay behind to do the handover of signals kit. A few others were staying behind also.

The rest of the squadron left early on the 25th. They landed in the dark by helicopter in Sangin. The guys were operating within an area that we call an Ops Box – basically an area on the map which people know we are operating in – going through compounds, clearing the area.

There was a really high IED threat up there, so the squadron picked a really difficult route through irrigated fields and not going along main tracks where you are pretty much guaranteed to find IEDs.

There was a lot of Taliban chatter on the radios, with stuff like, 'change the battery packs, they are coming', and all that general sort of stuff. So the lads were really wary about this, and so was the boss.

The guys on the ground were telling me when they got back that they were counting down the hours, saying: 'I've got sixteen hours left until end of tour.' Then night-time came.

They heard over ICOM [radio set] that the Taliban were watching them from where they were, so they moved compounds that night. The Taliban woke up in the morning to find them gone.

The Fire Support Group were getting contacted with rounds going over their heads, RPGs landing around them, about 100 metres away, so quite close.

Around midday on the 26th they were told they were coming back that evening. End of Tour. That would be it.

As they were patrolling, a grenade was thrown over the wall by a Taliban. 'Woody' – Lance Corporal of Horse Jo Woodgate – took the brunt of the blast.

One of the other lads, 'Reggie', took a bit of shrapnel as well.

When it happened, myself and Dave Dailey, the three bar, were up at Bastion Quarter-Masters' Stores trying to sort out some sigs kit for the handover.

We heard Op Minimise come over the loudspeakers – Op Minimise is when a Category A casualty is taken. To prevent other members of the casualty's unit informing the family before the military can track them down and give them a clear informative account of the precise situation, all communications are shut down. I turned to Dave and said: 'I hope it's not one of our guys.'

He said: 'Don't worry, it won't be.'

We got back and they told us that two of our guys had been hit. They said it was Woody and one other. At least one was Cat A. Cat A means critically injured and many guys are Cat A, but come through, so it wasn't over. I went for a cigarette and the Padre joined me.

I saw the Padre get called over by the QM [Quartermaster] – he was smoking as well. I knew something wasn't right because he had quit.

We got back into the vehicle and headed back to the compound. As we pulled in, one of the troop sergeants said: 'Don't get out of the truck, get back in.' He told us that Woody was dead.

We went straight up to the hospital to get some more information. We found out that Reggie was stable, that he was in theatre, but that he was going to be ok.

It was all a big shock, there were some tears and the rest of it. It wasn't good at all.

He was a really liked guy and everyone said it, but it was genuinely true. He was a really good guy. Really keen. He loved doing his job.

The guys on the ground didn't find out he was dead until they came back in off the ground that same night. Everyone was in shock, we all felt numb, exhausted and gutted.

The following day we had a service led by the Fijians, similar to the one for Foxy. There were readings, the OC read a poem and then the Fijians sang a hymn.

It was emotional, the song was so beautiful. The harmony of them singing; big tough Fijians but really beautiful voices.

I could feel my eyes starting to water. The corporal major said to us all: 'If you want to cry, you can, we are in our compound. He's a good friend, just let it go if you want to', and some of the guys did.

It just shows he was a really good lad and he will be missed. After that we returned to work.

We had the vigil and the repatriation ceremony. At around half twelve, we were all lined up on the flight line and as Woody got carried on to the Herc., it was incredibly emotional as well, because you see the coffin going past and you know that he's actually lying in that coffin. It's a weird feeling.

For the last few days we've just been handing over kit. Things like that, getting everything sorted; making sure the compound is clean, accounting for everything. Just getting rid of everything on our flicks and making sure the new guys coming in know what they are doing.

Yesterday we got called together. It was almost a day off – or as near as you'll get to one out here. And the OC said: 'Foxy's funeral is happening right now.' He said a few words about him, about his family. And we had another minute's silence.

In the afternoon we played troop volleyball. One of the guys came out wearing just a pair of red boxers, nothing else, with sides rolled up. He looked like a porn star prancing about on the volleyball court. We had music going, it was a good atmosphere.

Other than that, guys are getting back into the routine of doing phys, going to the gym.

Today we were getting squared away for the medals parade that is happening in a couple of weeks' time. Our OC wants the medals parade to be informal rather than marching about. I think he's done that because Benny – Guardsman 'Benny' Bennett – lost a leg a month or so back and this way he can be a part of it. It's a really good idea, really thoughtful.

A lot of people have made plans for what they'll do when they get back. They talk about it a lot. Everyone is talking about how this time is just dragging so much.

When everyone came in from the final op, you would have thought everyone would be happy, but the fact that Woody died, everyone was devastated. Everyone was thinking this was the last op. Why is someone dying on the last day before we become non-operational? Everyone was really cut up about that.

But it boils down to, we have a job to do and as bad as it may sound, Woody died doing the job he loved doing and he will never be forgotten.

It's been a difficult tour. We have had three people killed in action and many more who have been injured, including one, Barni, who managed to finish a patrol on foot despite having a broken ankle, which is pretty amazing. At least twice, people have had binoculars shot from their hands.

But we've got a lot to be proud of. We have achieved so much in just six months. The boundaries have been pushed.

The colonel of The Household Cavalry Regiment spoke to us the other day. He told us that we had set the standard for all other BRFs to follow. That we had reset the boundaries of what can be achieved. This is what LD, Foxy and Woody will be remembered for.

This is what we joined to do and what we get paid for. And we're doing it for the right reasons. Large parts of Afghanistan are safer now because of what we have done.

People can move about. They can go to the market. They can send their children to school. Some people back home are uncomfortable that people like us actually enjoy what we do.

As long as we do it for reasons like that, then we can't go far wrong.

◣ 4 Mechanized Brigade take control of UK forces in Helmand for Herrick 12

10 April 2010

Major Paul Smyth, RIFLES, Media Ops

The command of UK troops in Helmand province was officially handed over from 11 Light Brigade to 4 Mechanized Brigade today. The Transfer of Authority took place at Task Force Helmand Headquarters in Lashkar Gah when 11 Light Brigade, who have been in command for the last six months, lowered its flag over the base marking the end of their deployment.

Brigadier James Cowan of 11 Light Brigade said: 'I am immensely proud of every member of 11 Light Brigade. They have endured a difficult tour but shown courage and professionalism at every turn. Their successes have brought security and stability to many Afghan people.

'I want to pay particular tribute to the 61 members of the Brigade who made the ultimate sacrifice. We are all deeply saddened by their loss and they will live on in our memory. Also, our thoughts are with those who have suffered injuries in the line of duty.'

Brigadier Richard Felton of 4 Mechanized Brigade said: '11 Light Brigade have done a fantastic job over the last six months. We will build on the progress they have made here.

'All of 4 Mechanized Brigade are keen to start work and enthusiastic about the difference we can make to the ISAF mission and to the Afghan people.'

A ceremony to mark the Transfer of Authority was attended by Governor Mangal, the provincial Governor of Helmand.

He read a prepared statement in English thanking 11 Light Brigade for their efforts and saying that Brigadier Cowan and the servicemen and women in the Brigade would go down in Afghan history:

'None of your losses will have been in vain. You have worked hard to help the people of Afghanistan and we will never forget you.'

An Afghan
shepherd boy
watches the
British Army vet
inoculate his flock
of sheep. [Picture:
Major Paul Smyth]

Other titles published by Spellmount and The History Press

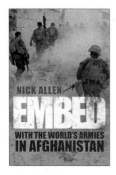

Embed: With the World's Armies in Afghanistan
Nick Allen

In the summer of 2007, English journalist Nick Allen quit a secure job in Pakistan to experience the daily life of foreign troops fighting the Taliban in Afghanistan. Over several years he journeyed as an embedded reporter with more than a dozen armies. *Embed* explores the fragile calm of Bamyan and its ancient sites and other so-called 'backwaters', together with the ferocious clashes of Helmand, Kandahar and other provinces.

978-0-7524-5889-2

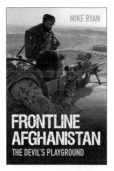

Frontline Afghanistan: the Devil's Playground
Mike Ryan

Following the success of his previous book, *Battlefield Afghanistan*, Mike Ryan looks at the state of this war-ravaged nation in 2009 when Barack Obama escalated America's military presence. With more than 200 colour photographs and analysis of the situation from those actually doing the fighting, *Frontline Afghanistan* may help the reader to make up his or her mind about the legitimacy of the conflict and the possible way forward.

978-0-7524-5248-7

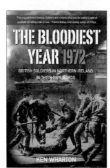

The Bloodiest Year: British Soldiers in Northern Ireland 1972, in Their Own Words
Ken Wharton

1972 was the bloodiest year of an already bloody conflict. Ken Wharton, a former soldier who did two tours of Northern Ireland, tells the story of the worst year of the Troubles through the accounts of the men who patrolled the streets of Belfast and Londonderry, who saw their comrades die and walked with death themselves.

978-0-7524-5906-6

Geordie: SAS Fighting Hero
Geordie Doran with Mike Morgan

Geordie Doran ranks as one of the most remarkable fighting soldiers of the twentieth century. He saw active service in Germany, Cyprus, the Korean War and Suez; he became an expert in jungle warfare in Malaya and in Borneo, as well as on key special operations in the deserts of Oman and Yemen, and Colonel Gaddafi's Libya. This is his story.

978-0-7524-6053-6

Visit our website and discover thousands of other History Press books.

www.thehistorypress.co.uk